# *Sunset*
# Pasta
# Cook Book

By the Editors of Sunset Books and Sunset Magazine

**Lane Publishing Co.** · **Menlo Park, California**

# Sunset shapes up pasta . . .

What's your favorite shape of pasta—long strands of spaghetti coated with a robust meat sauce? Tender ribbons of fettuccine? Squares of ravioli in a creamy tomato sauce?

We've organized this book by pasta shape, making it easy for you to find all the ways to sauce your favorite pasta.

All the recipes for spaghetti and other strand-shaped pasta are in one place—from old-fashioned spaghetti and meatballs to Indonesian bamie. In the ribbons chapter, you'll find fettuccine Alfredo, along with an international array of recipes for saucing ribbon-shaped noodles, proving that a noodle without a sauce is a noodle without a nation.

The squares and circles of ravioli, tortellini, won ton, and kreplach are together, as are elbow macaroni and the fancy shapes that add so much to casseroles and soups. There's even a chapter on pasta's close relatives (gnocchi, spaetzle, bean threads, rice sticks), and finally, an illustrated glossary of the many shapes and uses of pasta.

You'll learn how to make your own pasta, how to roll and shape the dough by hand or with a pasta machine. But if you don't feel like making your own, you can still enjoy the recipes, because the equivalent amount of packaged noodles is given.

By the way, don't hesitate to let your favorite pasta help keep *you* in shape. Figure about 100 calories for 4 ounces of plain, cooked pasta; then top it with a light, lean sauce such as the tangy tomato sauce pictured on the cover.

We wish to extend a special thank-you to those who helped with the research for this book: Antonio del Balzo and Chef Adelio Pagani of The Grand Hotel in Rome, and Gina Cappelli, Carlo A. DeVivo, Fran Hipp, Grace Nola, Adeline Schiro, Theresa Simoni, and Colin Tan. For their cooperation in sharing props for use in photographs, we also thank the Allied Arts Guild and the owners and staff at The Abacus, Taylor and Ng, William Ober Co., and Williams-Sonoma Kitchenware.

**Book Editors:**

Janeth Johnson Nix
Anne K. Turley

**Staff Researchers:**

Cynthia Scheer
Linda Brandt
Elaine R. Woodard

**Special Consultant:**

Linda Anusasananan
Assistant Editor, Sunset Magazine

**Photography:**

Tom Wyatt

**Photo Editor:**

Lynne B. Morrall

**Design:**

Cynthia Hanson

**Illustrations:**

The how-to art is by Carole Etow. Old prints are from Culver Pictures and Sedgewick Archives.

**Cover:**

Light, fresh Tangy Tomato Sauce (page 68) with Whole Wheat Pasta (page 8).

Editor, Sunset Books:
David E. Clark

First Printing April 1980

# Contents

## Special Features

# Making Pasta at Home

## How to Mix, Roll & Cut Pasta

This cook book is very easy to use. Because each shape of pasta has its own chapter, you can quickly see the many ways the same pasta can be transformed by different sauces. And you can take your choice of Italian, European, and Oriental treatments of similar pasta shapes.

For instance, if you need inspiration for that package of spaghetti in your cupboard, turn to the "Strands" chapter. There you'll find a treasury of recipes for strand-shaped pasta—and you may end up making a Greek or Indonesian dish.

This first chapter shows you how to make fresh pasta that can be rolled and cut into fettuccine, lasagne, ravioli, tortellini, cannelloni, and more.

Is making your own pasta worth the trouble? Yes. Most definitely, yes. Homemade pasta—with its tender, springy texture—tastes far better than dried, commercial pasta. It takes some practice and time to whip out those impressively long strands of pasta, but we think it's worth it.

Of course, you can't make every shape of pasta (the flat, medium-wide noodles are the most common), and there will probably be many occasions when packaged pasta is simply more convenient. Still, we encourage you to give homemade pasta a try. The all-purpose pasta dough recipe (page 8) is a good place to start, and you don't need any special equipment for it. You can knead the flour into a pliable dough without much effort and roll out the dough with a rolling pin.

If it seems like too much of a chore to hand-roll pasta, you can use mechanical aids instead. Pasta machines that knead dough, roll out strips, and cut them into noodles come in hand-crank and electric models.

## PASTA SCIENCE, PASTA ART

When you make pasta, you're living proof that a cook is part scientist, part artist. As scientist, you're aware that a certain amount of liquid added to flour activates gluten to produce a dough that can be pushed, patted, and rolled thin as paper. As artist, you sense the dough's progress toward noodlehood by touch and sight.

Why can't a scientific formula guarantee success? Because there are too many variables in flour and eggs that become apparent only when you begin to work the flour into dough. A food technologist can tell us the facts of flour—explaining that all-purpose flour is a blend of hard and soft wheat, and that it's hard wheat that has the highest protein count, the best gas-retaining properties to form elastic gluten, and the highest capacity for water absorption. But when it comes to 2 cups of flour and 2 eggs in a bowl in your kitchen, science gives way to your art as a pasta maker.

The directions for pasta making that follow are intended to encourage your pasta-making skills. Don't be alarmed if the same dough recipe turns out to be completely different on separate occasions. Neither dough will be "wrong," only in need of a little tender, loving attention in the form of more flour or more liquid. Look at it this way: pasta making is one of the few situations where grasping a few scientific facts allows you to demonstrate that science is not enough—at least in the kitchen.

And pasta making is fun. A hand-crank or electric pasta machine can be the star of a pasta party where everyone helps crank out fettuccine and has a grand time mixing and matching sauces for the heavenly light pasta. For suggestions on throwing a pasta party, see page 90.

## WHAT KIND OF NOODLES?

Homemade pastas have one thing in common: they're flat. With a rolling pin or pasta machine, they've been rolled out into thin sheets of dough and then cut into narrow or wide ribbons. Round strands (like spaghetti) or tubes (like macaroni), as well as most fancy shapes of pasta, can't be made at home. They're commercial products extruded through die-cut forms. And tiny alphabet letters: sorry, they can't be made at home either. There are many pasta shapes you can make with the basic dough recipes in this chapter. Fettuccine (medium-wide noodles), lasagne, cannelloni, and ravioli are just a few of them.

In addition, there's an eggless dough for Oriental noodles, and a recipe made with just the egg whites for noodles that are low in cholesterol and calories, but high in protein. Then there are recipes for whole wheat dough, semolina dough, and doughs made with corn, soy, buckwheat, and rye flours.

## GETTING STARTED

"The first step in pasta making is to drape your furniture with sheets." That's what a pasta-making aficionado told us. Comical as it sounds, finding a place to set long strips of thinly rolled dough is, indeed, one of the first steps in preparing pasta.

You need to plan space for about 16 feet of 4-inch-wide dough strips —the yield from one of this chapter's dough recipes when machine rolled. But avoid laminated plastic surfaces; dough tends to sweat and stick to them. Next, cover the space with tea towels or sheets, and flour them lightly.

Besides space for dough strips, you need a work surface—kitchen counter or table—that is a comfortable height for mixing and kneading dough.

**Equipment** is fairly simple. You can mix the dough in a large bowl or directly on your work surface. To mix the dough, you need a fork for stirring, plus a measuring cup and measuring spoons. To roll the dough out, you can use a pasta machine or rely on an arm-powered rolling pin.

You can use the blades that come with the pasta machine to cut dough strips into ribbons, or you can use a sharp knife. A large kettle to boil water and a pasta rake or colander complete the list of basic equipment for ribbon pasta.

**Ingredients** are very simple. Flour and liquid—that's all. The flour can be all-purpose, semolina, whole wheat, rye, or a mixture of flours, as suggested in the recipes. If you experiment with combinations of flours, remember that low-gluten flours, like corn and buckwheat, need to be mixed with a high-gluten flour, like all-purpose.

Most of our recipes call for 2 cups flour, 2 large eggs, and enough water to bind the dough. Some flours absorb more water than others, and some large eggs are larger than others. That means the total amount of water needed will vary.

## MIXING

We prefer a dough-mixing method that deliberately slows you down so you can control the proportion of liquid to flour. Think of it as the crater method. First you mound flour on a work surface or in a large bowl, then you make a well in the flour so it resembles a volcanic crater.

Next, break the eggs into the crater. With a fork, beat the eggs lightly as for an omelet, stir in a little water, and gradually draw flour from the sides of the crater with a circular mixing motion. Add a little more water and mix until the flour is moistened. If the dough is dry and crumbly, add a little more water. If it's sticky, sprinkle on a little more flour. When the dough gets stiff, use your hands.

There's no perfect dough. Some doughs are soft, some firm, depending on the amount of water you've worked into the dough. A soft dough (more water) is easier to roll with a rolling pin than a stiff dough. But a soft dough is difficult to roll in a machine because it sticks to the rollers.

If you mix dough on your work surface, clean the surface thoroughly before kneading. You'll probably have to scrape off bits of sticky dough with a knife or dough scraper. Dry your work surface and flour it lightly before kneading.

If you're using a heavy-duty mixer with a dough hook, put the flour, eggs, and 2 tablespoons of water into the mixer bowl. Mix enough to blend slightly. Add a little more water, if necessary, and then let the dough hook finish the mixing and most of the kneading. Remove the dough from the bowl and check the texture by kneading it a few times by hand on a lightly floured work surface. If you're using a food processor, see Food Processor Pasta (page 9).

## PUTTING A PASTA MACHINE TO WORK

Even if you own a pasta machine, a few minutes kneading the dough by hand before kneading it in the machine will improve its elasticity. Dough made with flours other than all-purpose flour may require considerable hand kneading before you put the machine to work.

Since brands of pasta machines differ slightly in size and function, the following directions are general. For instance, though all pasta machines have the same wringer-washer rollers that can be set wide apart, or closer together by degrees, each brand has labeled the roller positions differently. We, therefore, call the widest position the first setting.

**Kneading and rolling.** Cut the dough into four portions and roll out one portion at a time. (Keep unrolled portions covered.) Flatten the dough slightly, flour it, and then feed it through the widest roller setting. Fold the dough into thirds and feed it through the rollers again. Repeat the folding and rolling process 8 to 10 times or until the dough is elastic. If the dough feels at all damp or sticky, flour both sides each time it's rolled.

When the dough is smooth and pliable, set the rollers one notch closer together and feed the dough through. Flour the dough if it's damp or sticky. Repeat the rolling, setting the rollers closer each time, until the dough is a long strip as thin as you want it.

For medium-wide noodles (fettuccine) and thin noodles, stop rolling at the next to last setting. For lasagne, cannelloni, ravioli, and any other thick noodle, stop at the third to the last setting. Since machines differ, you may want to stop at a notch thicker or thinner.

Cut the strip in half crosswise for easy handling. Place the strip halves on a floured cloth or sheet and leave uncovered while you roll the remaining portions.

**Cutting by machine.** Let the strips dry for 5 to 10 minutes or until leathery but pliable. If you don't want to wait, be sure to flour both sides of a strip thoroughly, so the dough won't stick in the cutting blades and the noodles won't stick together.

Feed strips through the medium-wide blades for fettuccine, through the narrow blades for thin noodles (tagliarini or trenette). Some machines have attachments for wide and narrow lasagne, but lasagne can be cut easily by hand, as can ravioli and cannelloni. (See page 7 for lasagne, page 34 for ravioli , and page 52 for cannelloni.)

Lightly flour the cut noodles to keep the strands separate. Once cut, the noodles can be handled in either of two ways: you can toss them in a loose pile, or you can carefully gather the strands as they emerge from the machine (or have someone else catch them) and lay them in neat rows. The method you choose depends on the stickiness of the noodles and your temperament.

Since the point of making your own pasta is to enjoy freshly made noodles, it's best to cook them right away. You can make noodles slightly ahead of time, though, and leave the freshly cut pasta, uncovered, for as long as an hour before cooking it. If you make more noodles than you need, you can let them dry for 30 minutes to an hour (until they are dry but still pliable), then place them in a plastic bag and refrigerate for as long as 2 days, or freeze them for up to 2 months. Do not thaw before cooking.

Or you can dry the noodles thoroughly and store them indefinitely in airtight containers. You can impro-

vise a drying rack by setting a broom handle across two chairs. Drape the noodles over the handle and let them dry thoroughly. But handle carefully—homemade noodles tend to be extremely brittle when dried.

## PUTTING YOUR HANDS TO WORK

Pasta dough, like bread dough, needs friendly, warm hands to bring out its best qualities. Hand kneading, at least for a few minutes, is recommended for all pasta doughs. Resting is also important. Doughs made with all-purpose flour call for the least hand kneading and the shortest rest period because the gluten is fairly easy to activate.

**Kneading.** Begin by flattening the dough ball slightly. Fold the farthest edge of dough toward you. With your finger tips or the heel of your palm, press and push the dough away from you, sealing the fold. Rotate the dough a quarter-turn and continue the folding-pushing motion, making a turn each time. Work quickly with gentle, rhythmic kneading. If dough is sticky, sprinkle the work surface and dough ball with more flour.

Keep your eye on the dough rather than on the clock, and knead until the dough is smooth and elastic. Ten minutes seems to be the average time it takes to work all-purpose flour into pliable dough, though it's possible to knead vigorously and finish in half the time. The dough should have the firm bounce and velvety touch of a baby's bottom. If you cut it in half to check the texture, the inside should be pebbled with tiny air bubbles.

Cover the dough ball with an inverted bowl, or flour the dough ball and enclose it in plastic wrap. Then let it rest for about 20 minutes to further improve its elasticity.

**Rolling.** Start by cutting off one-fourth of the dough; keep the remaining dough covered. On a floured work surface, roll the dough out into a rectangle. For all-purpose

flour dough, each quarter portion should be rolled out to about 8 inches wide and 10 to 12 inches long for most noodles—the strip should be $\frac{1}{16}$ inch thick. Dough made with other flours will not roll as thinly as all-purpose flour dough.

If the dough is sticky, turn and flour both sides as you roll. Transfer the rolled strip to a lightly floured towel or sheet and leave it uncovered while you roll out the rest of the dough.

**Cutting.** Allowing rolled-out strips to dry for 5 to 10 minutes before cutting them is one way to make sticky dough cooperate. Be careful, though—it's easy to dry the strips too long; keep checking so they don't become brittle. Turn the strips over to dry briefly on both sides, and wait until they have the feel and flexibility of soft leather. Thickly rolled, moist dough strips drying in a cool, humid atmosphere are obviously going to dry more slowly than thinly rolled, low-moisture dough strips resting in a desertlike atmosphere.

Another way of assuring successful noodle cutting is to flour everything liberally—the cutting board, both sides of the strip, the cutting instrument, your hands, and even the noodles as soon as they're cut and the strands separated.

Cutting pasta by hand takes patience. However, no one is going to come along and measure your noodles, so don't worry about cutting them precisely $\frac{1}{4}$ or $\frac{1}{8}$ inch wide. And don't be overly concerned about the shape, either. Whatever shape you cut, intentional or unintentional, the Italians probably have a name for it—including *maltagliati*, which literally means "miscut" pasta. You could even tear thinly rolled strips into odd-shaped pieces and find that two separate cultures have already immortalized such a noodle: *straccia* (torn rags) in Sardinia and *turoscsusza* in Hungary. It's hard to be original—even with your mistakes —when cutting pasta.

*Medium-wide noodles (fettuccine).* Dry the rolled-out strips until they're leathery but very flexible.

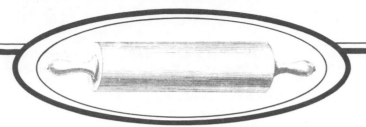

# How to Cook Pasta

Ask cooks why they boil pasta the way they do and they'll invariably answer, "My mother did it that way." Traditional ways to cook pasta are almost as numerous as the traditional ways to shape it. There's the boil-it-till-mushy school that has rightly fallen out of favor and been replaced by the Italian boil-it-al-dente tradition. Literally, *al dente* means "to the tooth"—tender but firm. And that's the way pasta tastes best. There's also the tradition that prescribes adding oil to the water because oil keeps the pasta from sticking together. It is countered by those who never add oil to the water because oil doesn't prevent stickiness.

There are also two time-honored ways to remove pasta from the pot. Generations have successfully used a spaghetti rake—a tool that looks like a wooden spoon with pegs sticking out of one side. Others drain pasta in a colander. If you enjoy the sound of clashing traditions, place in the same room a cook who always rinses pasta and one who never rinses pasta, and ask which method is best.

While testing our recipes, we also tested these various cooking methods. Our conclusions are part of the following step-by-step instructions for cooking pasta.

Start with a pot that will comfortably hold at least 3 quarts boiling water. (Water comes to a boil faster in a lightweight pot; a spaghetti cooker with a removable inner colander is a great convenience.)

Fill pot with 3 quarts water for each 2 cups (8 ounces) packaged dried pasta, or for 1 recipe fresh pasta. Add 1 tablespoon salt. Heat water to a rapid boil. For a pound of dried pasta, double the water and salt.

Add pasta slowly to the boiling water. Stir only if pasta needs to be separated, and then briefly.

For spaghetti that is too long for the pot, hold a bunch of it by one end and gently push the other end into the boiling water until the strands soften enough to submerge. The water should continue to boil. Plenty of continuously boiling water keeps pasta from sticking, but we did not find that adding oil prevented stickiness.

Boil pasta, uncovered, until al dente. How long does this take? The time depends on what kind of flour you use and whether the pasta is dried or fresh, as well as the pasta's size, shape, and thickness. Thin ribbons of fresh pasta made with all-purpose flour cook the fastest—just a minute or two. Thicker fresh pasta or pasta made with whole wheat, rye, or buckwheat takes 3 to 4 minutes.

Cooking times for packaged, dried pasta are usually printed on the package. Stand by the pot and start taste-testing before the recommended time is up.

Never cook pasta by the clock. It prefers your solicitous attention rather than the ticking of a kitchen timer. We find a spaghetti rake quite handy for dipping into the boiling pot and catching a strand or ribbon of pasta for testing.

Drain pasta as soon as it is al dente. There are a number of ways to get the job done. Use a spaghetti rake for strands or ribbons (not for macaroni or small pasta shapes), or drain pasta in a colander; or use a spaghetti cooker and just lift out the inner colander to drain. Select whichever method is fastest for you.

Run cold water over pasta only if you want to cool it for a salad, or want to cool lasagne or cannelloni so you can handle it. Pasta that will be served immediately should not be rinsed.

It is not necessary for pasta to drip dry thoroughly. Any excess water will blend with the sauce. Have a warm serving platter or plates—and your guests—ready and waiting.

---

Place a strip on a lightly floured cutting board and sprinkle with flour. Starting at the narrow end, roll up jelly roll fashion and cut into slices about ¼ inch wide. Unfurl the coiled noodles as soon as they are cut.

*Thin noodles (tagliarini, trenette).* Proceed as for medium-wide noodles, but cut in slices ⅛ inch wide.

*Lasagne.* There are two ways to cut lasagne. One method is to follow directions for medium-wide noodles, but cut the rolled strips into 2-inch-wide slices.

The second way makes fancier lasagne. Roll each quarter portion of dough into a rectangle about 12 by 16 inches. Using a fluted pastry wheel, cut dough into 2-inch-wide strips. Make each strip about 12 inches long, or whatever length conveniently fits your lasagne pan. (Remember, the lasagne will expand when cooked.) Separate the noodles and flour them so they won't stick together. If you follow the dimensions suggested, you'll end up with 32 lasagne strips. Dough that's rolled thicker yields fewer strips.

*Bows.* Called *farfalle* (butterflies) in Italian, bows are easy to make by hand. Proceed as for medium-wide noodles, but cut strips into 1-inch-wide noodles with a fluted pastry wheel. Cut noodles into 2 inch lengths. Pinch each noodle in the middle to make a bow shape.

*Cannelloni, ravioli, tortellini, cappelletti.* Directions for rolling and cutting cannelloni can be found on page 52. You will find directions for ravioli on page 34, tortellini and cappelletti on pages 43–45.

## ALL-PURPOSE PASTA

Using all-purpose flour, you can make a tender dough for all pasta purposes—noodles, lasagne, cannelloni, ravioli. The ingredients are as few and simple as the steps.

The amount of liquid that any flour can absorb varies with the moisture already in the flour, and with the temperature and humidity in your kitchen. The size of "large" eggs can vary, too. That's why there's really no way to tell how much water you'll need until you start working with the dough. But don't worry. Pasta dough graciously forgives most excesses. Too much water? Sprinkle on some flour and the dough will shape up quickly. Too heavy-handed with the flour? Add a little more water and the dough will become workable.

**2 cups all-purpose flour**
**2 large eggs**
**3 to 6 tablespoons water**
    **Additional all-purpose flour for
        kneading, rolling, and cutting**

Mound flour on a work surface or in a large bowl and make a deep well in center. Break eggs into well. With a fork, beat eggs lightly and stir in 2 tablespoons of the water. Using a circular motion, begin to draw flour from sides of well. Add 1 more tablespoon of the water and continue mixing until flour is moistened. If necessary, add more water, a tablespoon at a time. When dough becomes stiff, use your hands to finish mixing. Pat dough into a ball and knead a few times to help flour absorb liquid.

Clean and lightly flour the work surface. If you have a manual or electric pasta machine, knead dough by hand for 3 or 4 minutes, or until no longer sticky, before using machine. Sprinkle dough with flour, if needed. If you plan to use rolling pin, knead by hand for 10 minutes, or until smooth and elastic. Cover and let dough rest for 20 minutes.

With pasta machine or by hand, roll out one-fourth of the dough at a time to desired thinness. Keep unrolled portion covered. When all dough is rolled, cut strips into desired shapes by machine or by hand. Machine-rolled dough makes about 4 cups cooked pasta when machine-cut into medium-wide noodles, or about 32 pieces lasagne or cannelloni. Yield of hand-rolled noodles may vary.

## WHOLE WHEAT OR TRITICALE PASTA

Everybody has heard of whole wheat flour (sometimes called graham flour), but triticale is something new. Triticale looks and tastes exactly like what it is—a hybrid of wheat and rye. You can find it in most health food stores.

Noodles made with triticale are slightly darker than whole wheat noodles and have a more pronounced flavor. You can serve either kind of noodle with vegetable sauces, meat sauces, or just butter. All-purpose flour can be substituted for as much as half of the whole wheat or triticale for a softer, more elastic dough. If your whole wheat flour is stone ground, the dough will be especially dense.

**1¾ cups whole wheat or triticale
    flour**
**¼ cup toasted wheat germ**
**2 large eggs**
**3 to 6 tablespoons water**
    **Additional whole wheat flour
        for kneading, rolling, and
        cutting**

On a work surface or in a large bowl, combine flour and wheat germ. Mound flour on work surface and make a well in center. Break eggs into well. With a fork, beat eggs lightly and stir in 2 tablespoons of the water. Using a circular motion, begin to draw flour from sides of well. Add 1 more tablespoon of the water and continue mixing until flour is moistened. If necessary, add more water, a little at a time. When dough becomes stiff, use your hands to finish mixing. Pat into a ball and knead a few times to help flour absorb liquid.

Clean and lightly flour the work surface. If you have a manual or electric pasta machine, knead dough by hand for 5 to 10 minutes, or until no longer sticky, before using machine. Sprinkle with flour, if needed. If you plan to use a rolling pin, knead by hand for 10 to 15 minutes or until smooth and elastic. Cover and let rest for 20 minutes.

With pasta machine or by hand, roll out one-fourth of the dough at a time to desired thinness. Keep unrolled portion covered. This dough is best when rolled slightly thicker than all-purpose flour dough. If using a machine, stop rolling at third from thinnest setting for all pasta shapes. If rolling by hand, you'll find dough stiff, but try to roll each portion into $\frac{1}{16}$-inch-thick rectangles. Dough makes excellent noodles for lasagne even when rolled thicker.

When all dough is rolled, cut strips into desired shapes by machine or by hand. Machine-rolled dough makes about 3½ cups cooked pasta when machine-cut into medium-wide noodles, or about 25 pieces lasagne or cannelloni. Yield of hand-rolled pasta may vary.

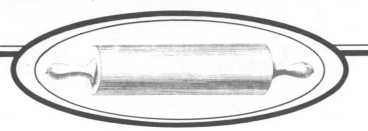

# FOOD PROCESSOR PASTA

A food processor reduces dough-mixing time to seconds. If you have a pasta machine as well as a food processor, you can whip out homemade noodles in about half an hour.

## ALL-PURPOSE FOOD PROCESSOR PASTA

2  **cups all-purpose flour**
2  **large eggs**
4  **tablespoons water**
   **Additional all-purpose flour for kneading, rolling, and cutting**

Using metal blade, process flour and eggs for 5 seconds or until mixture looks like cornmeal. With motor running, pour 4 tablespoons water down feed tube and process until dough forms a ball. Dough should be well blended, but not sticky. If it feels sticky, cut it into 3 pieces, sprinkle in a tablespoon of flour, and process again to form a ball. If dough looks crumbly, add another teaspoon or two of water to form dough. If food processor begins to slow down or stop—a good indication that dough is properly mixed—turn off motor and proceed to next step.

Turn dough onto a floured work surface and knead until smooth and elastic. (Mixing action of food processor reduces kneading time from 10 minutes to 2 or 3.)

If you intend to roll dough with a rolling pin, cover dough and let it rest for 20 minutes. If using a pasta machine, you can roll dough out immediately.

Roll out one-fourth of the dough at a time to desired thinness. Keep unrolled portion covered. When all dough is rolled, cut strips into desired shapes by machine or by hand. Machine-rolled dough makes about 4 cups cooked pasta when machine-cut into medium-wide noodles, or about 32 pieces lasagne or cannelloni. Yield of hand-rolled noodles may vary.

What follows is a roll call of dough recipes from this chapter that can be made in a food processor. For the most part, they're recipes that call for all-purpose flour; the recipes with rye, buckwheat,

triticale, semolina, and corn flour did not mix well when tested in a food processor.

The doughs should be mixed with the metal blade, and all should be kneaded by hand for a few minutes until they are smooth and elastic. If the dough feels sticky, cut it into 3 pieces, sprinkle in a tablespoon of flour, then process again to form a ball.

**Whole wheat pasta (page 8).** Follow the same steps as for all-purpose food processor pasta. After kneading by hand, allow dough to rest before rolling out in pasta machine or by hand. Stoneground whole wheat flour may be denser and more difficult to mix in a food processor.

**Spinach pasta (page 10).** Squeeze spinach and process with eggs until spinach is finely chopped. Add flour and process until dough forms a ball. You probably won't have to add water. Knead by hand for 2 to 3 minutes; if rolling out by hand, let rest for 20 minutes.

**Orange or rosy pasta (page 10).** Process strained carrots or beets with eggs just to mix, then add flour and process until dough forms a ball. Knead by hand for 2 to 3 minutes; if rolling out by hand, let rest for 20 minutes.

**Triple egg pasta (page 12).** Process egg yolks with 3 tablespoons of the water just until mixed. Add flour and process until dough forms a ball; if necessary add a little more water. Knead by hand for 2 to 3 minutes; let rest for 20 minutes.

**Low cal, high protein pasta (page 15).** Process egg whites and 3 tablespoons of the water just to mix, then add flour and, if necessary, a little more water. Knead for 2 to 3 minutes; let rest for 20 minutes.

**Eggless pasta (page 15).** Put flour in processor; then, with motor running, add water. Process until dough forms a ball. Knead for 2 to 3 minutes; let rest for 20 minutes.

**Soy pasta (page 15).** Proceed as for all-purpose food processor dough. Knead dough by hand for 5 to 10 minutes, incorporating more all-purpose flour if dough is sticky. Let dough rest for 20 minutes before rolling out with pasta machine (dough is difficult to roll out by hand).

## SPINACH PASTA

You can substitute green-tinted spinach pasta for plain pasta in many recipes. Whole wheat or semolina flour can replace all or part of the all-purpose flour. Whole wheat spinach dough will be more difficult to roll thinly than spinach pasta made with all-purpose flour or semolina. If you wish, use fresh spinach instead of frozen spinach. Cook enough to measure ¼ cup minced spinach.

**½ package (10-oz. size) frozen chopped spinach**
**2 cups all-purpose flour**
**2 large eggs**
**Additional all-purpose flour for kneading, rolling, and cutting**

Cook spinach according to package directions. Let spinach cool, then squeeze out as much liquid as possible. Mince finely. You should have ¼ cup spinach.

Mound flour on a work surface or in a large bowl and make a well in center. Break eggs into well. With a fork, beat eggs lightly and stir in the minced spinach. Mix with a circular motion to draw flour from sides of well. Continue mixing until flour is moistened. When dough becomes stiff, use your hands to finish mixing. Pat into a ball and knead a few times to help flour absorb liquid.

Clean and lightly flour the work surface. If you have a manual or electric pasta machine, knead dough by hand for 3 or 4 minutes, or until no longer sticky, before using machine. Sprinkle with flour, if needed. If you plan to use a rolling pin, knead by hand for 10 minutes or until smooth and elastic. Cover and let rest for 20 minutes.

With pasta machine or by hand, roll out one-fourth of the dough at a time to desired thinness. Keep unrolled portions covered. When all dough is rolled, cut strips into desired shapes by machine or by hand. Machine-rolled dough makes about 4 cups cooked pasta when machine-cut into medium-wide noodles, or about 32 pieces lasagne or cannelloni. Yield of hand-rolled pasta may vary.

## ORANGE OR ROSY PASTA

This homemade version of orange or rosy pasta isn't as brightly tinted as commercial rainbow-hued pasta. Commercial pasta makers use vegetable powders to color their dough. But since such powders aren't readily available, we use baby food—strained carrots for orange pasta and beets for rosy pasta (canned tomato paste can also be used).

**2 cups all-purpose flour**
**2 large eggs**
**3 tablespoons strained carrots or beets for babies or 3 tablespoons tomato paste**
**Additional all-purpose flour for kneading, rolling, and cutting**

Mound flour on a work surface or in a large bowl and make a deep well in center. Break eggs into well. With a fork, beat eggs lightly and stir in strained carrots or beets. Using a circular motion, begin to draw flour from sides of well. The strained vegetables should have enough liquid to moisten all the flour, but if dough is too crumbly to stick together, slowly add a few drops of water. When dough becomes stiff, use your hands to finish mixing. Pat into a ball and knead a few times to help flour absorb liquid.

Clean and lightly flour the work surface. If you have a manual or electric pasta machine, knead dough by hand for 3 or 4 minutes, or until no longer sticky, before using machine. Sprinkle with flour, if needed. If you plan to use a rolling pin, knead by hand for 10 minutes or until smooth and elastic. Cover and let rest for 20 minutes.

With pasta machine or by hand, roll out one-fourth of the dough at a time to desired thinness. Keep unrolled portion covered. When all dough is rolled, cut strips into desired shapes by machine or by hand. Machine-rolled dough makes about 4 cups cooked pasta when machine-cut into medium-wide noodles, or about 32 pieces lasagne or cannelloni. Yield of hand-rolled pasta may vary.

## SEMOLINA PASTA

Semolina flour makes superior pasta. It's milled from hard durum wheat, a special strain that exceeds all other wheat in protein and gluten content. Unfortunately, though, most semolina flour is shipped to commercial pasta makers. You may find some expensive, imported semolina in the gourmet sections of supermarkets, or you might find less expensive domestic-milled semolina in Italian grocery stores.

But don't even consider semolina if you hate kneading dough. Most semolina requires thorough hand kneading. Brands of semolina vary widely: some are very granular and take a half-hour of energetic kneading; others are less granular and take less attention. The final result is a butter-yellow pasta with a marvelously springy texture.

For variation, you can combine semolina with all-purpose flour to equal 2 cups. The more all-purpose flour you use, the easier it is to knead and roll the dough.

**2 cups semolina flour**
**2 large eggs**
**3 to 8 tablespoons water**
**All-purpose flour for kneading, rolling, and cutting**

Mound flour on a work surface or in a large bowl and make a deep well in center. Break eggs into well. With a fork, beat eggs lightly and stir in 2 tablespoons of the water. Using a circular motion, begin to draw flour from sides of well. Add 1 more tablespoon of the water and continue mixing until flour is moistened. If necessary, add more water, a little at a time. When dough becomes stiff, use your hands to finish mixing. Because semolina flour absorbs water more slowly than all-purpose flour, the dough may seem sticky when first mixed. Work with the dough, patting and kneading it into a ball, before deciding to cure the stickiness by adding more flour.

Clean and lightly flour the work surface. Knead by hand for 10 to 15 minutes or until smooth and elastic.

*(Continued on page 12)*

**1.** *Mound flour on a work surface or in a large bowl. Make a deep well and break eggs into well.*

**2.** *Use a fork to beat eggs lightly, as for an omelet; then mix in 2 tablespoons of the water. With a circular motion, begin to draw flour from sides.*

**3.** *Add another tablespoon of water and continue mixing. Add a little more water, if necessary, to moisten all the flour.*

**4.** *Use your hands to finish mixing when dough becomes stiff. Push and pat dough into a ball.*

**5.** *Fold and press dough to help flour absorb the liquid. If dough is sticky, sprinkle on a little flour; if dough is crumbly, drizzle on a little water.*

**6.** *Clean the work surface and flour it lightly, then knead dough until it's smooth, elastic, and no longer sticky.*

Cover and let dough rest for 30 minutes.

With pasta machine or by hand, roll out one-fourth of the dough at a time to desired thinness. Keep unrolled portion covered. When all dough is rolled, cut strips into desired shapes by machine or by hand. Machine-rolled dough makes about 4 cups cooked pasta when machine-cut into medium-wide noodles, or about 32 pieces lasagne or cannelloni. Yield of hand-rolled pasta may vary.

## BUCKWHEAT PASTA

Made from a mixture of buckwheat, whole wheat, and all-purpose flours, buckwheat dough produces chewy, strong-tasting noodles—definitely health food. A rich tomato sauce or chunky eggplant sauce (page 82) can complement buckwheat noodles for a meatless main dish.

**½ cup buckwheat flour**
**½ cup whole wheat flour**
**1 cup all-purpose flour**
**2 large eggs**
**3 to 6 tablespoons water**
     **Additional all-purpose flour for kneading, rolling, and cutting**

On a work surface or in a large bowl, combine flours. Push flour into a mound and make a well in center. Break eggs into well. With a fork, beat eggs lightly and stir in 2 tablespoons of the water. Using a circular motion, begin to draw flour from sides of well. Add 1 more tablespoon of the water and continue mixing until flour is moistened. If necessary, add more water, a little at a time. When dough becomes stiff, use your hands to finish mixing. Pat into a ball, sprinkle with flour, and knead a few times to help flour absorb liquid.

Clean and lightly flour the work surface. If you have a manual or electric pasta machine, knead dough by hand for 5 to 10 minutes or until no longer sticky. Cover and let dough rest for 20 minutes before using the machine. If you plan to use a rolling pin, knead by hand for 10 to

15 minutes or until smooth and elastic. Cover and let rest for 20 minutes.

With pasta machine or by hand, roll out one-fourth of the dough at a time to desired thinness. Keep unrolled portion covered. If using a machine, stop rolling at third from thinnest setting for all pasta shapes. If rolling by hand, you'll find dough stiff, but try to roll each portion into $\frac{1}{16}$-inch-thick rectangles.

When all dough is rolled, cut strips into desired shapes by machine or by hand. Machine-rolled dough makes about 3½ cups cooked pasta when machine-cut into medium-wide noodles, or about 25 pieces lasagne. Yield of hand-rolled noodles may vary.

## TRIPLE EGG PASTA

You'll fall in love with tender, rich noodles made from this dough. You may prefer the all-purpose dough recipe for Italian-type pasta, but keep this version in mind for your non-Italian pasta repertoire. It's irresistible when served with butter and a sprinkling of poppy seeds.

**2 cups all-purpose flour**
**3 egg yolks (large eggs), or 2 egg yolks and 1 whole egg**
**3 to 6 tablespoons water**

Mound flour on a work surface or in a large bowl and make a deep well in center. Place yolks in well. With a fork, beat yolks lightly and stir in 2 tablespoons of the water. Using a circular motion, begin to draw flour from sides of well. Add 1 more tablespoon of the water and continue mixing until flour is moistened. If necessary, add more water, a little at a time. When dough becomes stiff, use your hands to finish mixing. Pat into a ball and knead a few times to help flour absorb liquid.

Clean and lightly flour the work surface. If you have a manual or electric pasta machine, knead dough by hand for 3 or 4 minutes, or until no longer sticky, before using machine. Sprinkle with flour, if needed.

If you plan to use a rolling pin, knead by hand for 10 minutes or until smooth and elastic. Cover and let rest for 20 minutes.

With pasta machine or by hand, roll out one-fourth of the dough at a time to desired thinness. Keep unrolled portion covered. When all dough is rolled, cut strips into desired shapes by machine or by hand. Machine-rolled dough makes about 4 cups cooked pasta when machine-cut into medium-wide noodles, or about 32 pieces lasagne or cannelloni. Yield of hand-rolled noodles may vary.

## RYE PASTA

It's slightly unorthodox, but rye flour makes chewy-good noodles. Rye dough is stiffer than wheat dough, but still has enough gluten to be worked into pliable sheets of pasta—with some effort. Unless you have the arm strength of a professional masseuse, don't try to roll this dough with a rolling pin. Use a pasta machine. For variation—and for a softer dough—combine all-purpose flour with the rye to make the 2 cups.

**2 cups rye flour**
**2 large eggs**
**4 to 8 tablespoons water**
     **All-purpose flour for kneading, rolling, and cutting**

Mound flour on a work surface or in a large bowl and make a well in center. Break eggs into well. With a fork, beat eggs lightly and stir in 2 tablespoons of the water. Using a circular motion, begin to draw flour from sides of well. Add 2 more tablespoons of the water and continue mixing until flour is moistened. If necessary, add more water, a little at a time. When dough becomes stiff, use your hands to finish mixing. Pat into a ball and knead a few times to help flour absorb liquid.

Clean and lightly flour the work surface. Knead by hand for 15 to 20 minutes, sprinkling with flour as needed. When dough is pliable, cover and let rest for 20 minutes.

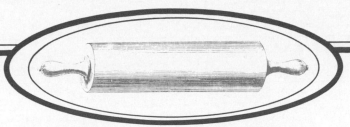

# What to Do When . . .

**. . . mixing dough on a work surface creates lumpy, half-mixed scraps.**
Don't try to knead them into the dough ball, just push scraps aside and discard. Next time, keep the back of the mixing fork in contact with the work surface as you draw flour into the egg mixture. That way, the fork acts as a scraper at the same time as it pulls flour from the bottom.

**. . . dough is sticky.**
Sprinkle dough and work surface with more flour and knead to incorporate the flour. Continue sprinkling with flour and kneading until dough is no longer sticky.

**. . . dough is crumbly.**
Add a little more water—carefully drizzle it over the dough—then use your hands to press and squeeze the dough into a ball before kneading.

**. . . you wonder if you've kneaded enough.**
Slice the dough ball in half with a sharp knife. The cross-section should be pebbled with tiny air bubbles. Alternatively, you can cut a portion off the dough and try to roll it out. If it rolls easily, without sticking, you've kneaded long enough.

**. . . there are large air bubbles in the dough.**
Knead it longer, either by hand or in a pasta machine. The machine's rollers usually squeeze out air bubbles. But don't worry if a few bubbles remain; the holes they leave in the dough when it's rolled thinly will give your noodles that hand-made look.

**. . . dough gets stuck in the roller or blades.**
Some pasta machines' rollers can be reversed. If the dough is not too tangled, sprinkle stuck dough with flour and try reversing the rollers. Otherwise, cut off unstuck portion of dough, take a stiff brush, and clean out the rollers or blades. Do not use water—most pasta machines will rust if cleaned with water.

To prevent further sticking, flour the dough strip on both sides each time it is rolled; also flour the rollers. Hold the dough straight when you feed it into the rollers. If necessary, cut the strip in half for easier handling.

To prevent dough strips from sticking in the cutting blades, let strips dry until they feel like chamois cloth. If you can't wait for them to dry, flour both sides of the strips before cutting. Sometimes you can feel the dough starting to stick and can thwart a disaster by sprinkling flour onto the rollers as the dough goes through.

If you've ruined one strip, it's easy to repair. Just fold it up again, reset the rollers at the widest position, and start rolling out the strip all over again.

**. . . dough comes out in a skinny strip.**
To stretch dough to the full width of the rollers, set rollers in widest position, fold dough in thirds, and feed the wider, folded side through the rollers. Repeat until dough reaches the full width of the rollers.

---

Work with one-fourth of the dough at a time; keep remaining dough covered. Knead in machine 6 to 10 times, then feed dough through rollers in succession from widest to third from thinnest setting. Sprinkle dough and rollers with flour as needed.

When all dough is rolled, cut strips into desired shapes with machine or by hand. This dough is best used for noodles or lasagne. Makes about 3½ cups cooked pasta when machine-rolled and cut into medium-wide noodles. Dough also can make about 25 strips lasagne.

## Corn Pasta

Be sure you use corn *flour* (found in health food stores), not corn meal. Noodles made with this dough have a mild corn flavor and very tender texture. The dough absorbs water slowly and is rather fragile. In fact, it's best to use a machine to roll it out.

**1 cup corn flour**
**1 cup all-purpose flour**
**2 large eggs**
**2 to 4 tablespoons water**
**Additional all-purpose flour for kneading, rolling, and cutting**

On a work surface or in a large bowl, combine flours. Mound flour and make a well in center. Break eggs into well. With a fork, beat eggs lightly and stir in 2 tablespoons of the water. Using a circular motion, begin to draw flour from sides of well. Add 1 more tablespoon of the

*(Continued on page 15)*

# Two Ways to Cut Pasta

## By machine

**1.** *Cut dough into 4 portions and roll out 1 portion at a time. Flatten dough slightly, flour it, then feed through widest roller setting.*

**2.** *Fold dough into thirds and feed again through widest roller setting. Flour both sides of dough if it's sticky. Repeat folding and rolling until dough is smooth and pliable.*

**3.** *Set rollers one notch closer together and feed dough through. Flour dough if it's sticky. Repeat the rolling, setting rollers closer each time, until dough strip is as thin as you want it. Repeat with remaining dough.*

## By hand

**4.** *Let rolled-out strips dry for a few minutes until they're like chamois cloth. Attach cutting blades to pasta machine and feed each strip through.*

**1.** *To roll by hand, flour the work surface and roll out one-fourth of the dough at a time. Roll it into a rectangle about 1/16 inch thick. If dough is sticky, turn and flour both sides as you roll.*

**2.** *To cut noodles by hand, let rolled-out strips dry for a few minutes until they're like chamois cloth. Flour strip and roll up, jelly-roll fashion, from the narrow end. Cut into slices as wide as you want the noodles.*

water and continue mixing until flour is moistened. If necessary, add more water, a little at a time. When dough becomes stiff, use your hands to finish mixing. Pat into a ball and knead a few times to help flour absorb liquid. Dough will be dense and sticky.

Clean and lightly flour the work surface. Knead by hand for 10 to 15 minutes, sprinkling with flour as needed. When dough is pliable, cover and let rest for 20 minutes. Work with one-fourth of the dough at a time; keep remaining dough covered. Knead in machine 4 or 5 times, then feed dough through rollers in succession from widest to third from thinnest setting. Sprinkle dough and rollers with flour as strips are rolled.

When all dough is rolled, cut strips into desired shapes with machine or by hand. This dough is best used for medium-wide noodles. Makes about 3½ cups cooked pasta when machine-rolled and cut into medium-wide noodles.

## SOY PASTA

Soy flour, found in most health food stores, adds protein to pasta. That's why soy pasta is such a good addition to a vegetarian diet. Soy flour lacks gluten, however, so the soy has to be mixed with all-purpose flour. The result is a dense, rather fragile dough that is much easier to roll out with a pasta machine.

**1 cup soy flour**
**1 cup all-purpose flour**
**2 large eggs**
**6 to 8 tablespoons water**
   **Additional all-purpose flour for
   kneading, rolling, and cutting**

In a large bowl or on a work surface, combine flours. Mound flour and make a well in center. Break eggs into well. With a fork, beat eggs lightly and stir in 2 tablespoons of the water. Using a circular motion, begin to draw flour from sides of well. Add more water, a tablespoon at a time, while continuing to mix.

When dough becomes stiff, use your hands to finish mixing. Pat and squeeze dough into a ball and knead a few times to help flour absorb liquid. Soy flour pasta takes more kneading than all-purpose pasta.

Clean and lightly flour the work surface. Knead by hand for 15 to 20 minutes or until smooth and elastic; cover and let rest for 30 minutes. With pasta machine, roll one-fourth of the dough at a time to desired thinness. Keep unrolled portion covered. In spite of the low gluten, this dough can be rolled to the next to the last setting. Makes about 3½ cups cooked pasta when machine-rolled and cut into medium-wide noodles.

## EGGLESS PASTA

Cholesterol counters, calorie watchers, or anyone on an eggless diet—here's your noodle. The bland but tender noodles made from this dough go well in Oriental soups or noodle dishes.

**2 cups all-purpose flour, or 1 cup
   all-purpose flour and 1 cup
   whole wheat flour**
**½ teaspoon salt (optional)**
   **About ½ cup warm water**
   **Additional all-purpose flour for
   kneading, rolling, and cutting**

In a large bowl, mix flour and salt (if desired). Slowly stir in enough of the warm water to make a stiff dough. Depending on what flour you use, you may not need the entire ½ cup water, or you may need slightly more.

Pat the dough into a ball and turn out onto a lightly floured work surface. Knead by hand for 10 to 15 minutes or until smooth and elastic. Sprinkle with flour, if needed. Cover and let rest for 20 minutes.

With pasta machine or by hand, roll out one-fourth of the dough at a time. Keep unrolled portion covered. Because this pasta is very tender, it is best to stop at the third to the last setting on a pasta machine. By hand, roll to about 1/16 inch thick.

When all dough is rolled, cut strips into desired shapes with machine or by hand. Use this dough for medium-wide or thin noodles. Makes about 4 cups cooked pasta when machine-rolled and cut into medium-wide noodles. Yield of hand-rolled noodles may vary.

## LOW CAL, HIGH PROTEIN PASTA

By eliminating just the egg yolks from pasta, you eliminate the cholesterol but keep the egg whites' protein. Eliminating the yolks also reduces the calories.

**2 cups all-purpose flour, or 1 cup
   all-purpose flour and 1 cup
   whole wheat flour**
**½ teaspoon salt (optional)**
**3 egg whites (large eggs)**
**3 to 6 tablespoons water**
   **Additional all-purpose flour for
   kneading, rolling, and cutting**

In a large bowl or on a work surface, mix flour and salt (if desired). In a small bowl, lightly beat together the egg whites and 3 tablespoons of the water. Mound the flour and make a well in center. Pour in the egg white mixture and, using a circular motion, begin to draw flour from sides of well. If dough seems crumbly, add more water, a tablespoon at a time. When dough becomes stiff, use your hands to finish mixing. Pat into a ball and knead a few times to help flour absorb eggs.

Clean and lightly flour the work surface. If you have a manual or electric pasta machine, knead dough by hand for 3 or 4 minutes, or until no longer sticky, before using machine. If you plan to use a rolling pin, knead by hand for 10 minutes or until smooth and elastic. Cover and let rest for 20 minutes.

With pasta machine or by hand, roll out one-fourth of the dough at a time to desired thinness. Keep unrolled portion covered. When all dough is rolled, cut strips into desired shapes by machine or by hand. This dough is best used for medium-wide or thin noodles. Makes about 4 cups cooked pasta. Yield of hand-rolled noodles may vary.

# Ribbons— Wide & Narrow

## LASAGNE, FETTUCCINE & OTHER FLAT NOODLES

The recipes in this chapter feature flat, ribbon-shaped noodles —fettuccine, lasagne, tagliarini— the kind most easily made with the pasta dough recipes in the previous chapter. You cut strips of thinly rolled dough into medium-wide ribbons for fettuccine, wide ribbons for lasagne, or narrow ribbons for tagliarini.

Of course, you don't have to make these noodles yourself to enjoy the wealth of recipes in this chapter. The comparable amount of packaged noodles is listed in each recipe's ingredients.

The most familiar ribbon-shaped noodles have Italian names—fettuccine actually means "little ribbons." Without sauce, though, fettuccine is a noodle without a nation: serve fettuccine with butter and poppy seeds and your guests will identify it as German; stir-fry cooked fettuccine with black bean sauce and the same noodles become Chinese; couch a paprika-flavored stew on a bed of noodles and you're in Hungary.

Throughout this section you'll spot traditional recipes from the Continent and the Orient, as well as Italian classics. You'll also find innovative pasta dishes that keep pace with today's taste for fresh ingredients combined in new ways. And we hope you'll be inspired to invent your own ribbon-shaped fresh noodle concoctions.

Beginning with such simple dishes as fettuccine with pine nuts, the recipes progress from cheese and vegetable-sauced noodles suitable for first courses, side dishes, and light meals, to heartier main-course noodle dishes, such as lasagne belmonte or lasagne swirls.

Many of the recipes take only minutes to prepare; others require more time. Often, though, the recipes that take the least time to prepare have to be served right away. We recommend presenting those dishes as separate courses, rather than side dishes. Have your guests or family seated as the noodles go into the boiling water; no one will mind waiting to applaud your virtuoso pasta performance. You can keep your captive pasta audience pacified with a salad or antipasto nibbles as you prepare the main noodle event.

If you're in the mood for a party and own a pasta machine, have a look at the special feature on staging a pasta party (page 90). There you'll find suggestions on timing, antipasto recipes, and a luscious quick tortoni for dessert.

## MARITATA SOUP

The Italian word *maritata* means "married woman," and in this soup we have a happy marriage of flavors—rich stock swirled with egg yolks, cheese, butter, and cream. Following a salad—like Belgian endive with a tart dressing—maritata soup can be served with French bread and featured as a main course. You can end the meal with baked winter pears, fresh strawberries, or melon, depending on the season.

**⅓ recipe triple egg pasta (page 12) or 3 ounces packaged tagliarini or vermicelli**
**½ cup (¼ lb.) sweet (unsalted) butter, softened**
**¾ cup grated Parmesan cheese**
**4 egg yolks**
**1 cup whipping cream**
**6 cups beef broth or chicken broth, or a combination of both**

Cut fresh pasta into thin noodles about 4 inches long, or break packaged noodles into 4-inch lengths.

Place butter, cheese, and egg yolks in a bowl and beat until creamy. Gradually beat in whipping cream.

In a 3-quart kettle, heat broth to boiling. Add noodles and cook in boiling broth until al dente (1 to 2 minutes for fresh noodles, or follow package directions). Stirring constantly, spoon small amount of hot broth into butter-cream mixture. Still stirring constantly, pour this mixture back into hot broth.

Immediately remove from heat. Ladle soup, including some of the noodles, into bowls. Makes 4 to 6 main-dish servings or 8 to 10 first-course servings.

## TAGLIARINI WITH GARLIC SAUCE

The aroma of six garlic cloves gently bubbling in olive oil leaves no doubt that this dish is for garlic lovers. But don't be deterred by all the garlic—it loses its pungency and mellows with slow cooking. In many recipes you can substitute salad oil for olive oil, but here we recommend using a light-flavored olive oil for an authentic Italian flavor.

**1 recipe all-purpose pasta (page 8) or 8 ounces packaged tagliarini**
**2 large tomatoes or 1 can (about 1 lb.) Italian-style tomatoes**
**¼ cup water**
**1 teaspoon dry basil**
**¾ teaspoon salt**
**¼ teaspoon *each* freshly ground black pepper and crushed red pepper**
**⅓ cup olive oil**
**6 large cloves garlic, minced or pressed**
**Boiling salted water**
**Grated Parmesan cheese**

Cut fresh pasta into thin noodles about 10 inches long.

Peel, seed, and coarsely chop tomatoes. If using canned tomatoes, break up with a spoon. In a bowl, combine tomatoes, water (omit if using canned tomatoes), basil, salt, black pepper, and red pepper; reserve. Place olive oil and garlic in a 1-quart pan. Cook, stirring occasionally, over medium-low heat until oil bubbles gently and garlic is a light gold. (Do not brown garlic or it will taste bitter.) Add tomato mixture to pan and simmer, uncovered, stirring occasionally, for 5 minutes.

Cook noodles in a large kettle of boiling salted water until al dente

(1 to 2 minutes for fresh noodles, or follow package directions). Drain noodles, then place in a serving bowl. Pour sauce over noodles, toss gently, then serve. Pass Parmesan cheese at the table. Makes 4 to 6 servings.

## FETTUCCINE WITH PINE NUTS

*(Pictured on page 19)*

In Italy, nut sauces with pasta are popular for festive occasions. You might offer this flavorful one as a choice at a pasta party (page 90) or toss it with noodles and serve as a side dish with grilled meat or fish. Butter is important in this recipe—don't substitute margarine.

**1 recipe all-purpose pasta (page 8) or 8 ounces packaged medium-wide noodles**
**4 tablespoons butter**
**½ cup pine nuts or slivered almonds**
**½ cup soft French-bread crumbs**
**1 small clove garlic, minced or pressed**
**2 tablespoons chopped parsley**
**Boiling salted water**

Cut fresh pasta into medium-wide noodles about 10 inches long.

In a small pan over low heat, melt butter. Add pine nuts, bread crumbs, and garlic and cook, stirring frequently, until nuts and crumbs are golden brown. Stir in parsley and cook for 30 seconds. Remove from heat.

Cook noodles in a large kettle of boiling salted water until al dente (1 to 2 minutes for fresh noodles, or follow package directions). Drain noodles, then place in a serving bowl. Pour nut mixture over noodles, then toss gently before serving. Makes 4 to 6 servings.

## FETTUCCINE RAPIDO

Italians joke about this sauce—it's for the housewife who's been so busy shopping she has little time left for cooking. *Rapido* implies the

kind of rapid cooking that calls for boiling the pasta water before you begin to make the sauce. Despite the simple ingredients, this is a spicy favorite with Italians and one of the popular items on the menu at the Grand Hotel in Rome.

**1 recipe all-purpose pasta (page 8) or whole wheat pasta (page 8), or 8 ounces packaged medium-wide noodles**
**2 small, dried, hot chile peppers, each broken in 3 pieces**
**⅓ cup olive oil**
**2 cloves garlic, minced or pressed**
**½ teaspoon salt**
**½ cup chopped parsley**
**Boiling salted water**

Cut fresh pasta into medium-wide noodles about 10 inches long.

In a small pan over low heat, cook chile peppers in olive oil until they begin to brown. Add garlic and cook for about 30 seconds more or just until limp (do not brown). Add salt and parsley and cook, stirring occasionally, for 1 minute longer. Remove from heat.

In a large kettle of boiling salted water, cook noodles until al dente (1 to 2 minutes for all-purpose noodles, 2 to 3 minutes for whole wheat noodles, or follow package directions). Drain noodles, then place in a serving bowl. Pour sauce over noodles, toss gently, then serve. Makes 4 to 6 servings.

## FETTUCCINE ALFREDO

Immortalized by Alfredo's restaurant in Rome, this is the recipe everyone thinks of when you say "fettuccine." It is very rich and so good! If you worry about the calories, enjoy it as a first course in small portions.

You'll have to serve this dish as soon as the last bit of cream is tossed with the noodles, because noodles are like sponges and they rapidly soak up the cream if allowed to stand. One way to make sure the fettuccine won't have to wait for your guests is to compose it in a chafing dish at the table.

*(Continued on next page)*

1 recipe all-purpose pasta (page 8) or 8 ounces packaged medium-wide noodles
Boiling salted water
6 tablespoons butter or margarine
1½ cups whipping cream
1 cup (3 oz.) grated Parmesan cheese
Salt and pepper
Whole or ground nutmeg

Cut fresh pasta into medium-wide noodles about 10 inches long. Cook noodles in a large kettle of boiling salted water until al dente (1 to 2 minutes for fresh noodles, or follow package directions). Drain.

While noodles are cooking, melt butter in a wide frying pan (or chafing dish, if you plan to assemble this at the table) over high heat until butter is lightly browned. Add ½ cup of the cream and boil rapidly until slightly thickened. Reduce heat to medium. Add noodles to sauce and toss gently. Then add half the cheese and ½ cup of remaining cream. Toss gently; repeat with remaining cheese and cream; toss again. Season with salt and pepper to taste and grate nutmeg generously over noodles (or use about ⅛ teaspoon ground nutmeg). Serve immediately. Makes 4 to 6 first-course servings.

## FETTUCCINE VERDE

A superb celebration of colors and flavors, fettuccine verde combines spinach pasta and green onions with a cream sauce for a variation on the fettuccine Alfredo theme. As with other cream-sauced noodles, you can't keep them waiting once they're ready to serve. The noodles soak up the sauce and the whole dish becomes gummy if allowed to cool. For a virtuoso dinner, serve your guests a melon wedge with a paper-thin slice of prosciutto; follow with fettuccine verde, then your main course, and a simple dessert such as dried figs and small chunks of imported Parmesan. For a light supper, serve fettuccine verde with grilled tomatoes and a tossed salad.

1 recipe spinach pasta (page 10) or 8 ounces packaged medium-wide green noodles
Boiling salted water
6 tablespoons butter or margarine
1 cup sliced green onions (including tops)
2 cloves garlic, minced or pressed
1 cup whipping cream
About 1½ cups grated Parmesan cheese
⅛ teaspoon ground nutmeg
Salt and pepper

Cut fresh pasta into medium-wide noodles about 10 inches long. Cook noodles in a large kettle of boiling salted water until al dente (2 to 3 minutes for fresh noodles, or follow package directions). Drain.

While noodles are cooking, melt butter in a wide frying pan over medium-high heat. Add green onions and garlic and cook, stirring, for 2 minutes. Add cream and heat until bubbling. Add hot noodles to pan and toss gently. Add ½ cup of the cheese and toss until noodles are evenly coated. Add another ½ cup cheese and toss again. Season with nutmeg and salt and pepper to taste, then toss again. Pass remaining ½ cup cheese at the table. Makes 4 servings.

## FETTUCCINE WITH LEMON & CREAM SAUCE

Elegant and uncomplicated, this simple first-course dish can be prepared in minutes. The lemon imbues the cream sauce with a refreshing flavor, and Italian parsley could be substituted for regular parsley for a more interesting flavor.

1 recipe all-purpose pasta (page 8) or 8 ounces packaged medium-wide noodles
Boiling salted water
1 cup whipping cream
2 tablespoons chopped parsley or Italian parsley
2 teaspoons grated lemon peel
Dash of salt
2 tablespoons butter, softened
2 tablespoons grated Parmesan cheese

Cut fresh pasta into medium-wide noodles about 10 inches long. Cook noodles in a large kettle of boiling salted water until al dente (1 to 2 minutes for fresh noodles, or follow package directions). Drain.

While noodles are cooking, place cream in a wide frying pan over medium-high heat and cook until bubbling. Add parsley, lemon peel, and salt, and cook for 30 seconds. Add hot noodles to cream mixture, reduce heat to low, and toss gently. Add butter and Parmesan cheese and continue tossing until noodles are evenly coated. Makes 4 servings.

## HAY & STRAW

Delighting in word pictures, the Italians call a combination of green and white noodles "hay and straw." They usually coat the noodles with a delicate sauce such as this combination of cream and fresh peas. It makes an excellent first course for a meal featuring a simple roast.

½ recipe spinach pasta (page 10) and ½ recipe all-purpose pasta (page 8), or 4 ounces *each* packaged green and white medium-wide noodles
2 pounds peas, shelled, or 1 package (10 oz.) frozen tiny peas, thawed
2 cups boiling water
Boiling salted water
2 tablespoons butter
⅛ teaspoon ground nutmeg
1 cup whipping cream
1 egg, beaten
½ cup grated Parmesan cheese
Parmesan cheese

Cut fresh pasta into medium-wide noodles about 10 inches long.

(Continued on page 20)

*Like a tricolored flag* from pasta lover's land, a platter of noodles shows off three favorites. Starting at the top, you see fettuccine-size whole wheat pasta (page 8), spinach pasta (page 10), and all-purpose pasta (page 8). They can be paired with any of the sauces—clockwise from the bottom, there's pine nut topping (page 17), zucchini sauce (page 23), and pesto (page 21).

Cook fresh peas in the 2 cups boiling water for 5 minutes (if you use frozen peas, cook for 2 minutes only); drain.

Cook noodles in a large kettle of boiling salted water until al dente (1 to 2 minutes for fresh noodles, or follow package directions). Drain noodles.

In a wide frying pan over medium-high heat, melt butter. Stir in nutmeg and cream. Add peas and noodles and quickly bring to a vigorous boil.

Remove pan from heat, stir in egg until blended; then mix in cheese. Serve at once and pass additional Parmesan cheese at the table. Makes 4 servings.

# FETTUCCINE A QUATTRO FORMAGGI

*(Pictured on page 22)*

Just reading the ingredients for this luscious dish can make you hungry. Three of the four cheeses—fontina, Bel Paese, and Gorgonzola—blend to make the grand duke of all cheese sauces. Parmesan, the fourth cheese, is tossed with the noodles and also passed around the table to be sprinkled on the finished dish. Fettuccine a quattro formaggi can be offered as a first course or served as an entrée, along with a crisp salad or vegetable vinaigrette. For dessert—a piquant Italian ice or fresh fruit.

**1 recipe all-purpose pasta (page 8) or 8 ounces packaged medium-wide noodles**
**3 tablespoons butter or margarine**
**1½ tablespoons all-purpose flour**
**⅛ teaspoon ground nutmeg**
**Dash of white pepper**
**1 cup half-and-half (light cream)**
**½ cup chicken broth**
**⅓ cup *each* shredded fontina and Bel Paese cheeses**
**⅓ cup crumbled Gorgonzola cheese**
**Boiling salted water**
**½ cup grated Parmesan cheese**
**Grated Parmesan cheese**

Cut fresh pasta into medium-wide noodles about 10 inches long.

In a 2-quart pan over medium

heat, melt 1½ tablespoons of the butter. Mix in flour, nutmeg, and pepper and cook, stirring, until bubbly. Remove pan from heat and stir in half-and-half and chicken broth. Return to heat and cook, stirring constantly, until it boils and thickens. Mix in fontina and Bel Paese cheeses; cook, stirring, until cheeses melt and sauce is smooth. Stir in Gorgonzola until blended; place pan over simmering water to keep sauce warm. Or, if made ahead, cool, cover, and refrigerate. To reheat, place over simmering water and stir until smooth and heated through.

Cook noodles in a large kettle of boiling salted water until al dente (1 to 2 minutes for fresh noodles, or follow package directions). Drain. Toss noodles lightly with remaining 1½ tablespoons butter and the Parmesan cheese. Spoon noodles onto serving plates. Top each serving with an equal amount of hot cheese sauce. Pass additional Parmesan cheese to sprinkle over individual servings. Makes 4 to 6 servings.

# FETTUCCINE WITH FISH

Here's another quick sauce for fettuccine. This one stretches a half-pound of fish to make four servings. With Italian noodle dishes, it is important not to drown the fettuccine in the sauce, but dress it with the sauce the way you would a salad. Italians prefer not to mix fish and cheese, but you might want to pass Parmesan cheese at the table.

**1 recipe all-purpose pasta (page 8) or 8 ounces packaged medium-wide noodles**
**1 small onion**
**¼ cup olive oil**
**1 can (about 1 lb.) Italian-style tomatoes**
**1 tablespoon chopped parsley**
**½ teaspoon *each* dry basil and salt**
**⅛ teaspoon freshly ground pepper**
**½ to ⅔ pound white fish fillets (halibut, turbot, rockfish, or sea bass), cut in 1-inch pieces**
**Boiling salted water**

Cut fresh pasta into medium-wide noodles about 10 inches long.

In a wide frying pan over medium-high heat, cook onion in olive oil until onion is limp. Coarsely chop tomatoes; save liquid for another use. Add tomatoes to pan along with parsley, basil, salt, and pepper. Reduce heat and simmer, uncovered, for 5 minutes. Add fish and continue cooking until fish is opaque throughout (about 7 minutes).

Cook noodles in a large kettle of boiling salted water until al dente (1 to 2 minutes for fresh noodles, or follow package directions). Drain noodles, then place in a serving bowl. Pour sauce over top and toss gently. Makes 4 servings.

# FETTUCCINE WITH SALAMI & MUSHROOMS

Chop up salami, combine it with sliced mushrooms, and you're on your way to making this family-pleasing main dish. Sautéed zucchini would make a good accompaniment, with perhaps a sherbet or Italian ice for dessert.

**1 recipe all-purpose pasta (page 8) or 8 ounces packaged medium-wide noodles**
**Boiling salted water**
**3 tablespoons butter or margarine**
**4 ounces dry salami, cut in ¼-inch cubes**
**½ pound mushrooms, thinly sliced**
**3 green onions, thinly sliced**
**⅓ cup half-and-half (light cream)**
**1 cup (3 oz.) grated Parmesan cheese**
**Freshly ground black pepper**

Cut fresh pasta into medium-wide noodles about 10 inches long. Cook noodles in a large kettle of boiling salted water until al dente (1 to 2 minutes for fresh noodles, or follow package directions). Drain.

While noodles are cooking, melt butter in a wide frying pan over medium-high heat. Add salami, mushrooms, and sliced onions; cook, stirring, until mushrooms are limp and pan juices have evaporated.

*(Continued on page 23)*

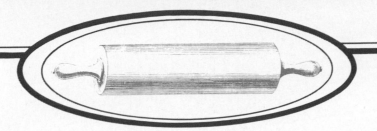

# Basil—An Herb for All Seasons

Basil is the reigning monarch of herbs in the mint family. The very name "basil" comes from the Greek word for king. But you don't have to be an herbalist or linguist to recognize culinary royalty—just sample the magnificent combinations of basil, Parmesan cheese, and oil that's called pesto.

We wouldn't limit basil to pesto, though. Basil is a superb addition to soups, salads, tomato-based sauces—any dish that calls for a sweet, spicy herb to add depth to the flavor. Fresh basil is best; next best is frozen basil; and least flavorful is packaged, dry basil. During the summer and early fall, many supermarkets carry fresh basil in the produce department. Of course, you won't have to depend on your grocer if you grow it yourself.

### Growing basil

You may find several kinds of basil in seed packets or as seedlings. The most common, officially called *Ocimum basilicum* is known as sweet basil or basilico. A summer annual, it grows to about 2 feet tall, with shiny green leaves that are 1 to 2 inches long, and with spikes of white flowers.

Growing basil requires warm soil and full sun. It should be planted in early spring when danger of frost is past. Space the plants 10 to 12 inches apart. Fertilize basil once during the growing season, but water regularly.

Basil tends to flower rather quickly, but when the plant starts putting out flowers, it decreases its leaf production. Since leaves are your objective, you'll want to increase leaf production by pinching out the flower stem. If you're vigilant about removing the flowers, you can harvest basil leaves throughout the growing season. But even kings are mortal: the first frost will kill basil.

### Long live the king

Freezing basil is the best and simplest way to preserve the herb. Just wash the leaves, pat off excess water, place the leaves in a single layer on a cooky sheet, and pop them into the freezer. When leaves are frozen, transfer them to plastic bags and return them to the freezer until needed. You don't have to thaw the leaves; they can be crumbled or chopped while frozen.

## Basil Parmesan

This mixture is delicious sprinkled on pasta dishes, tomatoes, salads, and soups.

**2 cups loosely packed fresh basil leaves, washed and thoroughly dried**
**1½ cups (4½ oz.) grated Parmesan cheese**

Place basil and Parmesan in a blender or food processor. Process with on-off bursts until mixture looks like green sawdust. Cover and refrigerate for up to a month, or freeze for longer storage. Scoop out spoonfuls as needed. Makes about 2 cups.

## Basic Pesto Sauce

*(Pictured on page 19)*

Originally, Genovese cooks used a mortar and pestle to grind the pesto ingredients to a smooth green paste. Our pesto sauce is made with speed and ease in a blender or food processor.

**2 cups lightly packed fresh basil leaves, washed and thoroughly dried**
**1 cup (3 oz.) grated Parmesan cheese**
**½ cup olive oil**

Place basil, Parmesan, and oil in a blender or food processor. Process until basil is finely chopped. Use pesto at once. Or place in small jars, adding a thin layer of olive oil to each jar to keep pesto from darkening; refrigerate for up to a week, or freeze for longer storage. Makes about 1⅓ cups.

**Garlic pesto.** Follow procedures for basic pesto but add 1 or 2 cloves **minced garlic.**

**Pasta with pesto.** To 4 cups hot, cooked, drained **fettuccine,** spaghetti, or similar pasta, add 6 tablespoons **pesto sauce** and 4 tablespoons softened **butter** or margarine; toss gently. Add 1 cup grated **Parmesan cheese** and mix. Serve additional Parmesan cheese and pesto to be added to taste. Makes 4 to 6 servings.

... Fettuccine with Salami & Mushrooms (cont'd.)

Reduce heat to low, add half-and-half, and heat through. Add hot noodles to pan and toss gently. Add cheese, half at a time, and toss until noodles are evenly coated. Sprinkle with pepper before serving. Makes 4 servings.

## GREEN NOODLES WITH BASIL & TOMATOES

Nothing accents the sweet ripeness of a tomato better than the pungent flavor of fresh basil. And nothing showcases this robust sauce better than tender ribbons of freshly made spinach noodles. (For other ways to enjoy fresh basil throughout the year, see page 21.)

**3 tablespoons olive oil or salad oil**
**1 large onion, chopped**
**¼ pound mushrooms, sliced**
**2 cloves garlic, minced or pressed**
**5 large ripe tomatoes, peeled, seeded, and coarsely chopped (about 4 cups)**
**¼ cup chopped parsley**
**⅛ teaspoon *each* marjoram leaves and pepper**
**1 teaspoon salt**
**½ teaspoon sugar**
**1 cup lightly packed fresh basil leaves**
**⅓ cup dry white wine**
**1 recipe spinach pasta (page 10) or 8 ounces packaged medium-wide green noodles**
**Boiling salted water**
**2 tablespoons butter or margarine, softened**
**Grated Parmesan cheese**

Heat olive oil in a wide frying pan over medium-high heat. Add onion, mushrooms, and garlic and cook,

*A generous grating of Parmesan, then a sauce made of fontina, gorgonzola, and bel paese add up to fettuccine a quattro formaggi—fettuccine with four cheeses. A light dusting of fresh nutmeg is the final fillip to this unforgettable dish. The recipe is on page 20.*

stirring, until liquid has evaporated. Add tomatoes, parsley, marjoram, pepper, salt, sugar, ½ cup of the basil, and wine. Bring to a boil; then reduce heat, cover, and simmer for 30 minutes. Uncover and cook rapidly, stirring, until sauce is reduced to about 3 cups; keep warm.

Meanwhile, cut fresh pasta into medium-wide noodles about 10 inches long. Just before serving, cook noodles in a large kettle of boiling salted water until al dente (2 to 3 minutes for fresh noodles, or follow package directions). Drain. In a shallow serving bowl, toss noodles lightly with butter, remaining ½ cup basil, and about 1 cup of the sauce. Top with remaining sauce. Pass Parmesan at the table. Makes 4 servings.

## NOODLES WITH CRISPY-MEAT SAUCE

When there's no time to shop and the larder is lean, how do you make a meal? With pasta and a bit of leftover meat, it's easy. Use a piece of cooked beef or pork to make this flavorful sauce, and garnish the pasta with fresh chopped tomatoes.

**1 recipe all-purpose pasta (page 8) or 8 ounces packaged medium-wide noodles**
**¼ cup olive oil**
**¼ cup butter or margarine**
**2 cups slivered cooked beef or pork roast**
**½ cup chopped parsley**
**1 teaspoon dry basil**
**½ teaspoon salt**
**¼ teaspoon *each* oregano leaves and pepper**
**Boiling salted water**
**2 tomatoes, chopped**
**Grated Parmesan cheese**

Cut fresh pasta into medium-wide noodles about 10 inches long.

In a wide frying pan over medium heat, combine olive oil and butter. Add meat and cook, stirring occasionally, until meat is crisp and browned (about 5 minutes). Add parsley, basil, salt, oregano, and pepper. Cook just until parsley begins to turn limp.

Cook noodles in a large kettle of boiling salted water until al dente (1 to 2 minutes for fresh noodles, or follow package directions). Drain noodles and turn into a shallow serving bowl. Spoon sauce over noodles and toss lightly. Garnish the top with tomatoes. Pass Parmesan cheese to sprinkle over individual servings. Makes 4 servings.

## GREEN NOODLES WITH ZUCCHINI SAUCE

*(Pictured on page 19)*

You can use any variety of summer squash to make this garden-fresh sauce for pasta. For a more substantial dinner you might accompany this pasta dish with a platter of cold cuts, olives, and wedges of feta or jack cheese.

**1 recipe spinach pasta (page 10) or 8 ounces packaged medium-wide green noodles**
**1 large onion, coarsely chopped**
**1 red bell or green pepper, seeded and coarsely chopped**
**1 clove garlic, minced or pressed**
**3 tablespoons olive oil or salad oil**
**1 can (about 1 lb.) Italian-style tomatoes**
**3 tablespoons chopped parsley**
**½ teaspoon *each* dry basil and marjoram leaves**
**¾ teaspoon salt**
**¼ teaspoon pepper**
**¼ cup dry red wine**
**3 medium-size (about 1 lb.) zucchini, crookneck, or patty pan squash, thinly sliced crosswise**
**Boiling salted water**
**Grated Parmesan cheese**

Cut fresh pasta into medium-wide noodles about 10 inches long.

In a wide frying pan over medium-high heat, cook onion, red pepper, and garlic in oil until vegetables are limp. Add tomatoes and their liquid (break up tomatoes with a spoon), as well as parsley, basil, marjoram, salt, pepper, and wine. Stirring, bring to a boil; then reduce heat, cover, and simmer for 30 minutes. Stir in zucchini and cook, covered, until crisp-tender (5 to 7 minutes).

Cook noodles in a large kettle of boiling salted water until al dente (2 to 3 minutes for fresh noodles, or follow package directions). Drain noodles, then place in a serving bowl. Spoon sauce over noodles, toss gently, then serve. Pass Parmesan cheese to sprinkle over pasta. Makes 4 servings.

## NOODLES WITH CABBAGE

*(Pictured on page 30)*

Here's a fresh idea for a side dish: toss delicate shreds of crisp-cooked cabbage with noodles. The contrasting textures are a delight. It takes only a few minutes to cook this pretty dish. We like to serve it alongside poached or broiled salmon, but it can complement any simple fish, poultry, or meat entrée.

**1 recipe all-purpose pasta (page 8) or 8 ounces packaged wide noodles**
**1 teaspoon salt**
**4 cups shredded cabbage**
**6 tablespoons butter or margarine**
**2 teaspoons sugar**
**½ teaspoon caraway seeds**
**¼ teaspoon pepper**
**Boiling salted water**

Cut fresh pasta into wide noodles about 4 inches long.

Sprinkle salt over cabbage, toss lightly, and let stand for 30 minutes. Squeeze cabbage to release liquid; discard liquid.

Melt butter in a wide frying pan over medium-high heat. Add cabbage, sugar, caraway seeds, and pepper. Cook, stirring occasionally, until cabbage is crisp-tender (about 5 minutes). Keep warm.

Cook noodles in a large kettle of boiling salted water until al dente (1 to 2 minutes for fresh noodles, or follow package directions). Drain, then toss with cabbage mixture before serving. Makes 6 servings.

## RYE NOODLES REUBEN

No, this isn't a culinary joke! It's a tasty variation of favorite "deli" flavors—only the shape has changed. For an unusual quick lunch or light dinner, serve rye noodles Reuben with a tossed salad. If you can't find packaged rye or whole wheat noodles, look for rye or whole wheat spaghetti in a health food store. Or make your own—they're the best.

**1 recipe rye pasta (page 12) or 8 ounces packaged rye or whole wheat medium-wide noodles**
**Boiling salted water**
**1 tablespoon butter or margarine**
**¼ pound lean pastrami or corned beef, cut in strips**
**1 can (8 oz.) sauerkraut, drained**
**1 tablespoon Dijon mustard**
**1 teaspoon caraway seeds**
**1 cup (4 oz.) shredded Swiss cheese**

Cut fresh rye pasta into medium-wide noodles about 10 inches long. Cook noodles in a large kettle of boiling salted water until al dente (3 to 4 minutes for fresh noodles, or follow package directions). Meanwhile, in a wide frying pan over medium heat, melt butter. Add pastrami strips and cook until heated through. Add sauerkraut, mustard, and caraway seeds. Cook and stir until heated through. Drain noodles and toss them with the sauerkraut mixture in the frying pan. Remove from heat. Toss with cheese and serve immediately. Makes 4 to 6 servings.

## CORN NOODLES CON QUESO

Corn noodles won't replace tortillas, but they can replace plain noodles when you want an easy, south-of-the-border side dish or light supper. You can buy corn noodles at some health food stores, or you can make your own.

Though it's tempting to roll fresh noodles into extravagant lengths to show off your skill with a pasta ma-

chine, the noodles for this recipe should be cut into 4 to 6-inch lengths: these shorter noodles won't tangle when tossed with the other ingredients. Keep serving dishes and plates warm and have everyone seated when the noodles go into the boiling water—this dish takes only minutes.

**1 recipe corn pasta (page 13) or 8 ounces packaged medium-wide corn noodles**
**Boiling salted water**
**2 tablespoons butter or margarine**
**1 can (7 oz.) chopped green chiles**
**1 cup (4 oz.) shredded jack cheese**

Cut fresh pasta into medium-wide noodles, 4 to 6 inches long. Cook noodles in a large kettle of boiling, salted water until al dente (2 to 3 minutes for fresh noodles or follow package directions). Meanwhile, melt butter in a wide frying pan over low heat. Add chiles and heat through. Drain noodles and toss with butter and chiles in frying pan. Remove from heat and toss in cheese. Serve immediately. Makes 4 to 6 servings.

## SAVORY BAKED NOODLES

Served as a side dish or as a separate course, this is an irresistible baked noodle dish. Its origins go back to the savory Russian version of kugel, the noodle pudding well known in Jewish households.

**1 recipe spinach pasta (page 10) or 8 ounces packaged medium-wide green noodles**
**Boiling salted water**
**¾ pint (1½ cups) large curd cottage cheese**
**1 cup sour cream**
**1 clove garlic, minced or pressed**
**3 green onions (including tops), thinly sliced**
**1 teaspoon Worcestershire**
**¼ teaspoon liquid hot pepper seasoning**
**2 tablespoons butter or margarine, melted**
**½ cup grated Parmesan cheese**

Cut fresh pasta into medium-wide noodles about 4 inches long. Cook noodles in a large kettle of boiling salted water until al dente (2 to 3 minutes for fresh noodles, or follow package directions). Drain, rinse with cold water, and drain again.

In a bowl, combine cottage cheese, sour cream, garlic, sliced onions, Worcestershire, liquid hot pepper seasoning, and melted butter. Gently stir in noodles. Turn mixture into a greased 1½-quart casserole. Sprinkle Parmesan cheese over top. Bake, covered, in a 350° oven until heated through (about 30 minutes). Makes 6 servings.

## OLD-FASHIONED CHICKEN & NOODLES

Sometimes known as chicken pot pie, this recipe is a Pennsylvania Dutch specialty. Thick, square, homemade noodles soak up some of the rich chicken broth for a hearty meal-in-a-bowl, perfect for supper on cold winter nights.

    1 recipe all-purpose pasta
      (page 8)
    1 broiler-fryer chicken (about 3
      lbs.), cut in serving-size
      pieces
    6 small whole onions, peeled
    4 tablespoons butter or
      margarine
    7 cups water
    1½ teaspoons salt
    ⅛ teaspoon white pepper
    2 carrots, cut in 1-inch lengths
    2 stalks celery, cut in 1-inch
      lengths
      Chopped parsley

Roll out pasta dough to thickness of strips for lasagne; cut into 2-inch squares. In a 6-quart kettle over medium-high heat, melt butter. Brown chicken and onions in butter until golden on all sides. Add water, salt, and pepper; reduce heat, cover, and simmer for 15 minutes. Add carrots and celery and continue cooking, covered, until chicken and vegetables are tender (about 40 minutes). Remove chicken pieces from kettle and keep warm. Spoon off excess fat from broth. Bring liquid to a rapid boil; add noodle

squares and cook until al dente (4 to 6 minutes).

Serve in shallow soup bowls. Place a piece of chicken and some vegetables, noodles, and broth in each; sprinkle with parsley. Makes 4 to 6 servings.

## APRICOT KUGEL

Sweet kugels (noodle puddings) are often included in festive menus during the Jewish High Holy Days. This version is rather light and not overly sweet. At a *Sunset* taste panel, even those who claimed they never like noodle puddings asked for second helpings.

    1 recipe all-purpose pasta (page
      8) or 8 ounces packaged
      medium-wide noodles
      Boiling salted water
    ⅔ cup dried apricots
    3 eggs
    1 cup large curd cottage cheese
    ½ cup sour cream
    4 tablespoons butter or
      margarine, melted
    ¼ cup sugar
    1½ teaspoons vanilla
    1 teaspoon *each* ground cin-
      namon and grated lemon
      peel
    ¼ teaspoon ground nutmeg
    ½ teaspoon salt
    1 cup soft bread crumbs
    ¼ cup walnuts or almonds,
      finely chopped

Cut fresh pasta into medium-wide noodles about 4 inches long. Cook noodles in a large kettle of boiling salted water until al dente (1 to 2 minutes for fresh noodles, or follow package directions). Drain, rinse with cold water, and drain again.

Barely cover apricots with boiling water. Let stand for 15 minutes; drain and finely chop.

In a bowl, beat eggs. Stir in cottage cheese, sour cream, 2 tablespoons of the melted butter, sugar, vanilla, cinnamon, lemon peel, nutmeg, salt, and apricots. Gently stir in noodles. Turn mixture into a buttered 8-inch-square baking pan.

In a frying pan over medium heat,

cook bread crumbs and nuts in remaining 2 tablespoons melted butter until crumbs are golden. Sprinkle over top of noodles. Bake, uncovered, in a 375° oven for 30 minutes or until heated through and top is golden brown. Serve warm or at room temperature. Makes 6 servings.

## BAKED CHICKEN WITH WHOLE WHEAT NOODLES

For a special occasion, serve baked chicken on thin ribbons of garlicky whole wheat noodles. If you prefer not to make fresh pasta, use packaged tagliarini, spaghetti, or linguine in place of the noodles.

    1 recipe whole wheat pasta (page
      8) or 8 ounces packaged
      tagliarini, spaghetti, or
      linguine
    1 broiler-fryer chicken (about 3½
      lbs.), cut into pieces
      Salt and pepper
    ½ teaspoon *each* rosemary and
      thyme leaves
    2 cups Italian mushroom gravy
      (page 69) or 1 can (about
      15 oz.) marinara sauce
    3 cloves garlic, minced or pressed
    ¼ cup butter or margarine
    ½ teaspoon *each* oregano leaves
      and onion powder
      Boiling salted water

Cut fresh pasta into thin noodles about 10 inches long.

Sprinkle chicken with salt, pepper, rosemary, and thyme. Place, skin side down, in a greased baking pan. Bake in a 375° oven for about 20 minutes. Baste with some of the mushroom gravy; bake for 10 minutes longer. Turn, skin side up, and baste with more gravy. Basting several times, bake for about 25 minutes longer or until meat near bone is no longer pink when slashed.

In a wide frying pan over medium heat, cook garlic in butter, stirring often, until garlic is a light gold. Mix in oregano and onion powder. Cook noodles in a large kettle of boiling salted water until al dente (2 to 3 minutes for fresh noodles or follow package directions). Drain noodles, then add to garlic-butter mixture and toss well to mix.

Turn noodles into a rimmed serving platter; arrange chicken pieces on top. Heat the remaining mushroom gravy to pass at the table. Makes 4 or 5 servings.

## CITRUS CHICKEN WITH NOODLES

Even when you start with uncooked chicken, this delicious entrée for two takes only 30 minutes to assemble. After grating the orange peel, you might cut out the orange sections and add them to a tossed green salad to serve alongside.

½ **recipe all-purpose pasta (page 8) or 4 ounces packaged medium-wide noodles**
1 **whole chicken breast (about 1 lb.), split**
½ **cup water**
¼ **cup slivered almonds**
2 **tablespoons butter or margarine**
½ **teaspoon grated orange peel**
¼ **teaspoon grated lemon peel**
½ **to ¾ cup sour cream**
½ **teaspoon salt**
⅛ **teaspoon white pepper**
  **Boiling salted water**
1 **tablespoon chopped parsley**

Cut fresh pasta into medium-wide noodles about 4 inches long.

Place chicken in a 2-quart pan, add water, and bring to a boil. Reduce heat, cover, and simmer until chicken is tender (about 20 minutes).

Strain broth and reserve. When chicken is cool enough to handle, discard skin and bones and cut chicken into 1-inch squares.

Meanwhile, lightly brown almonds in 1 tablespoon of the butter and set aside. Return boned chicken to cooking pan with remaining 1 tablespoon butter, orange peel, lemon peel, sour cream, salt, pepper, and ¼ cup of the chicken broth. Stir lightly and heat; do not boil.

Cook noodles in a large kettle of boiling salted water until al dente (1 to 2 minutes for fresh noodles, or follow package directions). Drain, then add noodles to chicken mixture and stir lightly. Spoon into a serving dish; top with almonds and parsley. Makes 2 servings.

## HUNGARIAN GOULASH WITH NOODLES

According to food expert George Lang, Americanized goulashes shouldn't happen to a Rumanian. But the New World often transforms Old World recipes to suit its own palate, thereby creating its own traditions. Serving goulash with noodles is an American tradition that we enjoy. If anyone complains about the lack of authenticity when you serve this savory stew, just wink and claim it's an old Rumanian recipe handed down from your Swedish grandmother.

3 **large onions, thinly sliced**
3 **tablespoons salad oil**
1 **teaspoon caraway seeds**
½ **teaspoon marjoram leaves**
1 **teaspoon salt**
1 **tablespoon paprika**
2 **pounds boneless beef chuck, cut in 1-inch cubes**
1 **cup dry red wine**
1 **recipe all-purpose pasta (page 8) or 8 ounces packaged wide noodles**
  **Boiling salted water**
2 **tablespoons butter or margarine**
2 **tablespoons chopped parsley**

In a 4 or 5-quart kettle over medium heat, cook onion, stirring occasionally, in 1 tablespoon of the oil until

onion is limp. Stir in caraway seeds, marjoram, salt, and paprika. Remove onion from pan and set side.

Increase heat to medium-high and brown meat, half at a time, adding the remaining 2 tablespoons oil as needed. Return meat to pan along with onion. Pour in wine and bring to a boil; then reduce heat, cover, and simmer until meat is tender (about 1½ hours).

Meanwhile, cut fresh pasta into wide noodles about 4 inches long. Just before serving, cook noodles in a large kettle of boiling salted water until al dente (1 to 2 minutes for fresh noodles, or follow package directions). Drain noodles and toss with butter and parsley. Mound noodles in center of serving dish. Spoon meat mixture around noodles. Makes 4 to 6 servings.

## NOODLES & BEEF WITH BLACK BEAN SAUCE

We've taken liberties with this succulent Chinese dish. Fresh rice noodles are the typical pasta used, but all-purpose pasta or soy flour pasta, cut in 4-inch lengths, makes a delicious substitute. It's important to stop cooking the noodles while they're still firm to the bite, because they're cooked a second time in a wok.

The black beans used as a seasoning are small fermented black beans preserved in salt. They're sold in Oriental markets, packaged in small plastic bags. Tightly covered, they'll keep almost indefinitely at cool room temperature. These beans have a very pungent odor, but when cooked, they impart a flavor that is appealing to even the most conservative taste.

*(Continued on page 28)*

*Served in ducal splendor* is this thrifty dish of marrow-filled veal shanks called osso buco. It has a zesty topping of parsley, garlic, and grated lemon peel. The recipe is on page 29.

½ **recipe all-purpose pasta (page 8) or soy pasta (page 15), or 4 ounces packaged medium-wide noodles**
  **Boiling salted water**
4 **tablespoons salad oil**
½ **pound boneless lean beef**
1 **teaspoon** *each* **cornstarch, dry sherry, and soy sauce**
1 **tablespoon water**
  **Cooking sauce (directions follow)**
2 **tablespoons fermented black beans, rinsed, drained, and finely chopped**
2 **large cloves garlic, minced or pressed**
1 **teaspoon minced fresh ginger**
¼ **teaspoon crushed red pepper**
1 **green pepper, seeded and cut in 1-inch squares**
2 **green onions (including tops), cut in 1-inch lengths**

Cut fresh pasta into medium-wide noodles about 4 inches long. Cook noodles in a large kettle of boiling salted water until al dente (1 to 2 minutes for fresh all-purpose noodles, 2 to 3 minutes for fresh soy noodles, or follow package directions). Drain, rinse with cold water, and drain again. Toss noodles with 1 tablespoon of the oil.

Cut beef with the grain into 1½-inch-wide strips. Cut each strip across the grain in ⅛-inch-thick slanting slices. In a bowl combine cornstarch, sherry, soy, and water. Add beef and stir to coat. Stir in 1½ tea-

spoons of the oil; let stand for 15 minutes to marinate.

Prepare cooking sauce and set aside.

Heat a wok or wide frying pan over high heat. When pan is hot, add 1 tablespoon of the oil. Add noodles and stir-fry until heated through. Remove noodles from pan.

Add remaining 1½ tablespoons oil to pan. When oil begins to heat, add black beans, garlic, ginger, and red pepper; stir once. Add beef and stir-fry for 2 minutes. Add green pepper and green onions and continue stir-frying for 1 minute, adding a few drops of water if vegetables stick to pan. Stir cooking sauce, add to pan, and cook, stirring, until sauce boils and thickens. Add noodles to pan and toss lightly to mix. Makes 2 or 3 servings.

**Cooking sauce.** In a bowl combine ½ cup **water** and 1 tablespoon *each* **cornstarch** and **soy sauce**.

# BEEF STROGANOFF WITH NOODLES

Beef Stroganoff is a good make-ahead main dish. You can bake the beef and mushroom mixture and refrigerate or freeze it, then reheat and stir in the sour cream when ready to serve. The noodles, of course, should be cooked at the last minute.

2 **pounds round steak, cut 1 inch thick**
  **About 3 tablespoons salad oil**
1 **teaspoon salt**
¼ **teaspoon pepper**
¼ **cup dry red wine**
½ **pound small whole onions, peeled**
½ **pound mushrooms, sliced**
1 **clove garlic, minced or pressed**
3 **tablespoons flour**
1 **can (10½ oz.) consommé**
4 **tablespoons tomato paste**
1 **bay leaf**
1 **recipe all-purpose pasta (page 8) or 8 ounces packaged medium-wide noodles**
  **Boiling salted water**
½ **cup sour cream**
2 **tablespoons chopped parsley**

Cut meat across the grain in ¼-inch-thick slices. In a wide frying pan over medium-high heat, brown meat, half at a time, in about 1½ tablespoons of the oil. Transfer meat to a 3-quart casserole. Add salt, pepper, and wine.

Add another 1½ tablespoons oil to pan and cook onions over medium heat, stirring frequently, until golden. Add mushrooms and garlic and cook until mushrooms are limp. With a slotted spoon, transfer vegetables to casserole.

Blend flour into drippings in frying pan; cook, stirring, until flour is golden. Remove from heat and gradually stir in consommé and tomato paste. Return to heat and bring to a boil, stirring; then pour over meat. Add bay leaf, cover, and bake in a 350° oven until meat is tender (about 1½ hours). If made ahead, cool, cover, and refrigerate (or freeze, for longer storage); then reheat when needed.

Cut fresh pasta into medium-wide noodles about 4 inches long. Just before serving, cook noodles in a large kettle of boiling salted water until al dente (1 to 2 minutes for fresh noodles, or follow package directions). Drain noodles and spoon into center of a rimmed serving dish. Stir sour cream into meat mixture, then spoon meat, vegetables, and sauce over noodles. Sprinkle with parsley. Makes 4 to 6 servings.

# NORWEGIAN MEATBALLS WITH WHOLE WHEAT NOODLES

You can match your meatballs with your noodles when you make this northern European version of meatballs and spaghetti. For medium-wide noodles, make walnut-size balls. For thin noodles, make smaller meatballs. The sweet, nutlike flavor of whole wheat noodles complements the Scandinavian spices in the meatballs. You could substitute plain noodles, though, if you prefer them.

2 slices white bread
¾ cup milk
2 pounds lean ground beef
¼ pound ground pork
1½ teaspoons salt
¼ teaspoon *each* pepper, ground
     allspice, and ground ginger
1 egg
4 tablespoons butter or
     margarine
1 medium-size onion, sliced
¼ cup all-purpose flour
2 cups water
     Salt and pepper
1 recipe whole wheat pasta
     (page 8) or 8 ounces pack-
     aged whole wheat noodles
     Boiling salted water

Remove and discard crusts from bread. Tear bread into coarse crumbs; moisten with milk and let stand for 5 minutes. Combine beef, pork, salt, pepper, allspice, ginger, and egg. Add bread and knead mixture thoroughly for 2 minutes. (This kneading makes a fine-grained, tender meatball.) With wet hands, roll meat mixture into walnut-size balls, or even smaller if you wish.

In a wide frying pan over medium-high heat, melt 2 tablespoons of the butter. Add meatballs, a portion at a time, and brown them on all sides. Using a slotted spoon, transfer meatballs, as browned, to a 2-quart casserole. Repeat until all meatballs are browned. Pour off all but 1 tablespoon pan drippings; reserve remaining drippings.

Add onion to the 1 tablespoon pan drippings and cook, stirring occasionally, until onion is limp. Spoon onion over meatballs.

Return 2 tablespoons of the reserved drippings to pan; add flour and cook, stirring, over low heat until flour is golden brown. Gradually pour in water and cook, stirring, until gravy is smooth and thickened. Season to taste with salt and pepper. Pour gravy over meatballs. If made ahead, cover and refrigerate until next day. Bake, covered, in a 350° oven for 45 minutes (55 minutes if refrigerated).

Meanwhile, cut fresh pasta into medium-wide or thin noodles about 8 inches long. Just before serving,

cook noodles in a large kettle of boiling salted water until al dente (2 to 3 minutes for fresh noodles, or follow package directions). Drain noodles, then toss with remaining 2 tablespoons butter. Mound noodles in center of serving dish. Spoon meatballs and gravy around noodles. Makes 6 servings.

## O SSO BUCO

*(Pictured on page 27)*

Braised veal shanks, with their succulent treasure of marrow in the bones, are a superlative accompaniment for buttered pasta. You can buy special spoons to scoop out the marrow, though the tip of a knife will do the job, too.

Cooked in the style of Milan, osso buco is garnished with a mixture of lemon peel, garlic, and parsley.

7 to 8 pounds meaty slices of
     veal shanks with marrow in
     the bone, cut through the
     bone in 2-inch-thick slices
     (12 to 18 pieces)
     Salt and all-purpose flour
½ cup butter or margarine
1½ cups dry white wine
¾ to 1 cup chicken broth
1½ tablespoons grated lemon peel
½ cup chopped parsley
1 clove garlic, minced or
     pressed
1 recipe all-purpose pasta (page
     8) or 8 ounces packaged
     medium-wide noodles
     Boiling salted water

Sprinkle shanks with salt, roll shanks in flour, and shake off any excess flour. In a large heavy kettle over medium heat, melt 6 tablespoons of the butter and brown shanks, a portion at a time, on all sides; remove and set aside. When all shanks have been browned, return meat to pan and add wine and ¾ cup of the broth. Cover and simmer for 1½ to 2 hours or until meat is very tender when pierced. At this point you can cool, cover, and refrigerate until next day, if you wish. Reheat slowly when ready to continue.

Combine lemon peel, parsley, and garlic; reserve.

Cut fresh pasta into medium-wide noodles about 10 inches long. Cook noodles in a large kettle of boiling salted water until al dente (1 to 2 minutes for fresh noodles, or follow package directions). Drain noodles and toss with remaining 2 tablespoons butter. Arrange meat on a platter, surround meat with noodles, and keep hot. Scraping browned particles free, bring sauce to a rolling boil; add a little more broth if needed. Add half of lemon-garlic mixture to sauce and let simmer for 2 minutes; garnish meat with remaining lemon-garlic mixture. Pour sauce over meat and noodles. Makes 6 to 8 servings.

## S CHWEINSPFEFFER WITH NOODLES

If you like sauerbraten, you'll adore schweinspfeffer (literally, peppered pork). As with sauerbraten, the longer the cubes of pork marinate, the more authentically German the flavor. Don't discard the marinade—some of it goes into the gravy for a piquant sauce. The sauce is thinner than the gravy in other meat-and-noodle recipes, though, so we like to pour it over the noodles to toss and mix together, and serve the tender pork cubes separately.

2 cups dry red wine
1 cup *each* cider vinegar and
     water
1 *each* onion and carrot, coarsely
     chopped
1 clove garlic, minced or pressed
½ teaspoon thyme leaves
¼ teaspoon sage leaves
1 teaspoon salt
½ teaspoon whole black peppers
2 to 2½ pounds boneless pork
     butt, cut into 1½-inch cubes
2 tablespoons butter or
     margarine
2 teaspoons sugar
2 tablespoons all-purpose flour
1 can (10½ oz.) beef bouillon
1 recipe all-purpose pasta (page
     8) or 8 ounces packaged
     medium-wide noodles
     Boiling salted water

Place wine, vinegar, water, onion, carrot, garlic, thyme, sage, salt, and

*(Continued on page 31)*

*... Schweinspfeffer with Noodles (cont'd.)*

whole peppers in a 2-quart pan. Bring to a boil, then pour over meat. Cool, cover, and refrigerate for 1 day or for as long as 3 days.

Remove meat from marinade and pat dry with paper towels. Strain marinade and reserve. Melt butter in a wide frying pan over medium-high heat. Add meat, a portion at a time, and brown quickly on all sides. Using a slotted spoon, transfer meat to a 3-quart pan. Stir sugar and flour into pan drippings and cook, stirring, over low heat until flour has turned golden brown. Gradually pour in bouillon and ⅔ cup of the reserved marinade and cook, stirring, until gravy is smooth and slightly thickened. Pour gravy over meat. Cover pan and simmer until meat is tender (about 1½ hours).

Meanwhile, cut fresh pasta into medium-wide noodles about 4 inches long. Just before serving, cook noodles in a large kettle of boiling salted water until al dente (1 to 2 minutes for fresh noodles, or follow package directions). Drain noodles, then toss with part of gravy. Spoon onto a platter and surround with meat and remaining gravy. Makes 6 servings.

## LASAGNE BELMONTE

Mystery surrounds the origin of lasagne, the widest of the pasta noodles, but we know it inspired the invention of layered casseroles, today found in all parts of Italy. Each region of Italy seems to have its own variation, though. This version most closely follows the traditional style of southern Italy which uses tomato and beef sauce and several flavorful cheeses. For a spicier casserole you can substitute Italian sausage for part of the beef.

*Noodles with cabbage, a refreshing contrast in textures and colors, is one of those delightfully easy-to-make side dishes that can steal the spotlight even from whole poached salmon. The recipe is on page 24.*

1 medium-size onion, chopped
3 tablespoons olive oil or salad oil
1½ pounds lean ground beef or 1 pound lean ground beef and ½ pound Italian sausage
1 clove garlic, minced or pressed
2 cans (8 oz. *each*) tomato sauce
1 can (6 oz.) tomato paste
½ cup *each* dry red wine and water
1 teaspoon *each* salt and oregano leaves
½ teaspoon *each* pepper and sugar
½ recipe all-purpose pasta (page 8) or 12 to 16 packaged lasagne noodles
Boiling salted water
2 cups (1 lb.) ricotta cheese or small curd cottage cheese
8 ounces mozzarella cheese, thinly sliced
½ cup grated Parmesan cheese

In a wide frying pan over medium-high heat, cook onion in olive oil until onion is limp; add beef and garlic and cook, stirring, until meat is brown and crumbly. (If using sausage, remove casings, chop sausage, and brown with beef.) Spoon off and discard excess fat. Stir in tomato sauce, tomato paste, wine, water, salt, oregano, pepper, and sugar. Cover pan and simmer for about 1½ hours.

While sauce cooks, cut fresh pasta into wide strips (about 12 inches long) for lasagne. You'll need 12 to 16 pieces. Cook noodles in a large kettle of boiling salted water until al dente (3 to 4 minutes for fresh noodles, or follow package directions). Drain, rinse with cold water, and drain again.

Butter a 9 by 13-inch baking dish. Spread a thin layer of sauce over the bottom. Arrange ⅓ of the noodles in an even layer over sauce. Spread ⅓ of the sauce over noodles; dot with ⅓ of the ricotta, then cover with ⅓ of the mozzarella. Repeat this layering two more times. Sprinkle Parmesan cheese over top. If made ahead, cover and refrigerate.

Bake, uncovered, in a 350° oven until hot and bubbly (40 to 50 minutes). Cut into squares to serve. Makes 8 servings.

## CHICKEN LASAGNE

Lasagne is a good choice for entertaining. A make-ahead dish, it can be assembled a day in advance—or longer if you wish to freeze it—then heated just before serving. For an easy meal, serve this creamy chicken lasagne with slices of melon and clusters of grapes.

3 pounds chicken breasts, split
3 cups water
½ cup butter or margarine
1 pound mushrooms, sliced
½ cup dry white wine
½ teaspoon tarragon leaves
4 tablespoons all-purpose flour
1 teaspoon salt
¼ teaspoon *each* white pepper and ground nutmeg
2 cups half-and-half (light cream)
½ recipe all-purpose pasta (page 8) or 12 to 16 packaged lasagne noodles
Boiling salted water
¾ pound Swiss or Gruyère cheese, shredded

Place chicken in a 4-quart pan, add water, and bring to a boil. Reduce heat, cover, and simmer until chicken is tender (about 20 minutes). Strain broth and reserve. When chicken is cool enough to handle, discard skin and bones and shred chicken. You should have about 5 cups cooked meat.

In a wide frying pan over medium-high heat, melt 4 tablespoons of the butter. Add mushrooms and cook, stirring, until mushrooms are limp. Add wine and tarragon, reduce heat to medium, and cook until most of the pan juices have evaporated; set aside.

In a 2-quart pan over medium heat, melt remaining 4 tablespoons butter. Blend in flour, salt, pepper, and nutmeg and cook, stirring, until bubbly. Remove pan from heat and gradually stir in half-and-half and 2 cups of the reserved chicken broth. Save remaining broth for other uses. Return pan to heat and cook, stirring, until smooth and thickened. Stir mushrooms into sauce.

Cut fresh pasta into wide strips (about 12 inches long) for lasagne.

*(Continued on next page)*

You'll need 12 to 16 pieces. Cook noodles in a large kettle of boiling salted water until al dente (2 to 3 minutes for fresh noodles, or follow package directions). Drain, rinse with cold water, and drain again.

Butter a 9 by 13-inch baking dish. Spread a thin layer of sauce over the bottom. Arrange ⅓ of noodles in an even layer over sauce. Spread ⅓ of chicken over noodles, top with ⅓ of sauce, then cover with ⅓ of cheese. Repeat this layering two more times, ending with a cheese layer. If made ahead, cover and refrigerate.

Bake, uncovered, in a 350° oven until hot and bubbly (40 to 50 minutes). Cut into squares to serve. Makes 8 servings.

---

## GREEN LASAGNE BOLOGNESE

A rich meat sauce coupled with a delicate nutmeg-flavored white sauce is culinary marriage, Italian-style. This meat sauce has more beef than the Italian original, yet it remains faithful to the seasonings of northern Italy.

**¼ pound chicken livers (optional)**
**1 *each* large carrot, large onion, and celery stalk, all finely chopped**
**2 tablespoons olive oil or salad oil**
**2 pounds lean ground beef**
**½ pound cooked ham, coarsely chopped**
**1 clove garlic, minced or pressed**
**4 tablespoons canned tomato paste**
**2 teaspoons dry basil**
**½ teaspoon salt**
**⅛ teaspoon pepper**
**1 large can (1 lb. 12 oz.) Italian-style tomatoes**
**½ recipe spinach pasta (page 10) or 12 to 16 packaged green lasagne noodles**
**Boiling salted water**
**Warm white sauce (directions follow)**
**3½ to 4 cups (10½ to 12 oz.) grated Parmesan cheese**

Coarsely chop chicken livers and set aside.

In a large pan over medium-high heat, cook carrot, onion, and celery in oil until onion is limp. Remove vegetables with a slotted spoon and set aside. Add beef and cook until browned and crumbly. Spoon off and discard excess fat. Mix in ham, chicken livers (if used), and garlic; reduce heat to low and add cooked vegetables, tomato paste, basil, salt, pepper, and tomatoes with their liquid (break up tomatoes with a spoon). Simmer, covered, for 30 minutes; then uncover and cook, stirring often, until sauce is reduced to about 6 cups (about 30 minutes).

While meat sauce simmers, cut fresh pasta into wide strips (about 12 inches long) for lasagne. You'll need 12 to 16 pieces. Cook noodles in a large kettle of boiling salted water until al dente (3 to 4 minutes for fresh noodles, or follow package directions). Drain, rinse with cold water, and drain again. Prepare white sauce.

Stir meat sauce and white sauce together. Butter a 9 by 13-inch baking dish. Spread a thin layer of sauce over the bottom. Arrange ⅓ of noodles in an even layer over sauce. Spread ⅓ of sauce over noodles, then sprinkle ⅓ of Parmesan cheese on sauce. Repeat this layering two more times, ending with a cheese layer. If made ahead, cover and refrigerate.

Bake, uncovered, in a 350° oven until hot and bubbly (40 to 50 minutes). Cut into squares to serve. Makes 8 servings.

**White sauce.** In a small pan over medium heat, melt 2 tablespoons **butter** or margarine. Blend in 2 tablespoons **all-purpose flour** and ⅛ teaspoon ground **nutmeg.** Cook, stirring, until bubbly. Remove pan from heat and gradually stir in 1 cup **milk.** Return pan to heat and cook, stirring, until smooth and thickened.

---

## LASAGNE SWIRLS

Here's meatless magic with pasta. Instead of layering wide lasagne noodles in a baking dish, you wrap them around a low-fat, high protein ricotta cheese filling. The result is a dish that looks and tastes good.

**½ recipe all-purpose pasta (page 8) or 16 packaged lasagne noodles**
**Boiling salted water**
**2 packages (10 or 12 oz. *each*) frozen chopped spinach, thawed**
**2 cups (6 oz.) grated Parmesan cheese**
**2⅔ cups ricotta cheese**
**1 teaspoon *each* salt and pepper**
**½ teaspoon ground nutmeg**
**2 cloves garlic, minced or pressed**
**1 large onion, chopped**
**3 tablespoons olive oil or salad oil**
**2 large cans (15 oz. *each*) tomato sauce**
**¼ cup dry red wine**
**½ teaspoon *each* dry basil and oregano leaves**

Cut fresh pasta into wide strips (about 12 inches long) for lasagne. You'll need 16 pieces. Cook noodles in a large kettle of boiling salted water until al dente (2 to 3 minutes for fresh noodles, or follow package directions). Drain, rinse with cold water, and drain again.

Squeeze spinach to remove excess moisture. Mix spinach with 1½ cups of the Parmesan cheese, as well as ricotta, salt, ½ teaspoon of the pepper, and nutmeg. Spread about ¼ cup of this cheese mixture along entire length of each noodle; roll noodles up. Butter two 9 by 13-inch baking dishes. Stand rolled noodles on end in each dish so they do not touch.

In a wide frying pan over medium heat, cook garlic and onion in olive oil until onion is limp. Add tomato sauce, wine, basil, oregano, and remaining ½ teaspoon pepper. Simmer, uncovered, for 10 minutes. Pour sauce around noodles. If made ahead, cover and refrigerate.

Bake, covered, in a 350° oven until heated through (about 30 to 40 minutes). Remove from oven and sprinkle remaining ½ cup Parmesan cheese evenly over noodles. Makes 8 servings.

# VEGETABLE LASAGNE

Your guests may never even guess that this vegetable-laden lasagne is meatless. Whole wheat noodles and cheese make it a protein-rich entrée.

⅓ cup olive oil or salad oil
1 large onion, chopped
2 cloves garlic, minced or pressed
1 medium-size eggplant (about 1 lb.), diced, but not peeled
¼ pound mushrooms, sliced
1 can (about 1 lb.) Italian-style tomatoes
1 can (8 oz.) tomato sauce
½ cup dry red wine
1 medium-size carrot, shredded
¼ cup chopped parsley
2 teaspoons oregano leaves
1 teaspoon *each* dry basil and salt
¼ teaspoon pepper
½ recipe whole wheat pasta (page 8) or 12 to 16 packaged lasagne noodles
Boiling salted water
2 cups (1 lb.) ricotta cheese
2 cups (8 oz.) shredded mozzarella cheese
1½ cups (4½ oz.) grated Parmesan cheese

In a wide frying pan over medium heat, add olive oil. When oil is hot, add onion, garlic, eggplant, and mushrooms and cook, stirring frequently, for 15 minutes. Add tomatoes and their liquid (break up tomatoes with a spoon), tomato sauce, wine, carrot, parsley, oregano, basil, salt, and pepper. Bring to a boil, then reduce heat and simmer, covered, for 30 minutes. Uncover and continue cooking until sauce is thick. You should have 5 cups sauce; set aside.

Cut fresh pasta into wide strips (about 12 inches long) for lasagne. You'll need 12 to 16 pieces. Cook noodles in a large kettle of boiling salted water until al dente (3 to 4 minutes for fresh noodles, or follow package directions). Drain, rinse with cold water, and drain again.

Butter a 9 by 13-inch baking dish. Spread about ¼ of the sauce over the bottom. Arrange ⅓ of noodles in an even layer over sauce. Dot noodles with ⅓ of ricotta. Sprinkle over ⅓ of mozzarella, then sprinkle with ¼ of the Parmesan cheese. Repeat this layering two more times. Spread remaining sauce evenly over top and sprinkle with remaining Parmesan cheese. If made ahead, cover and refrigerate.

Bake, uncovered, in a 350° oven until hot and bubbly (40 to 50 minutes). Cut in squares to serve. Makes 8 servings.

# LASAGNE WITH CHEESE

We don't advise taking short cuts with this exceptional lasagne from Northern Italy—the fresh pasta is essential, but we think the effort is worthwhile. The meat in this recipe can do double duty. You start the tomato sauce by simmering a rump roast and then when the meat is tender you remove it to serve at another meal. Only the broth is used in the sauce. The result is a rich, flavorful lasagne that isn't overly filling.

2 whole cloves
½ small onion
2 tablespoons olive oil
2 tablespoons butter or margarine
3-pound boneless rump roast, cut in 4 pieces
⅓ cup dry white wine
1 large can (12 oz.) tomato paste
7½ cups water
1½ teaspoons salt
¼ teaspoon *each* pepper and ground nutmeg
½ cup loosely packed fresh basil leaves
¼ cup coarsely chopped celery tops
White sauce (directions follow)
½ recipe all-purpose pasta (page 8)
Boiling salted water
3 cups (12 oz.) shredded mozzarella cheese
1½ cups (4½ oz.) grated Parmesan cheese

Stick cloves into onion. Place olive oil and butter in a heavy 5 or 6-quart pan and place over medium-high heat. Add meat and onion and brown on all sides. Add wine and cook until most of the liquid has evaporated. Mix in tomato paste, water, salt, pepper, nutmeg, basil, and celery tops.

Bring to a boil, reduce heat, cover, and simmer until meat is nearly tender (about 2 hours). Uncover and continue cooking until meat is very tender (about 30 minutes). Remove meat to a covered casserole and keep warm if you plan to serve it soon, or save for another meal.

Increase heat to medium and cook sauce, stirring frequently, until reduced to about 4 cups. Strain sauce; reserve 3 cups sauce for lasagne and spoon 1 cup over meat.

Prepare white sauce and set aside.

Cut fresh pasta into wide strips (about 12 inches long) for lasagne. You'll need about 16 pieces. Cook noodles in a large kettle of boiling salted water until al dente (2 to 3 minutes for fresh noodles, or follow package directions). Drain, rinse with cold water, and drain again.

To assemble lasagne, butter a 9 by 13-inch baking dish. Place an even layer of noodles on the bottom. Spread noodles with ¼ of white sauce, then swirl in ¼ of tomato sauce. Sprinkle with mozzarella and Parmesan cheeses. Repeat this layering three more times, then end with a top layer of noodles sprinkled with about ¾ cup of the mozzarella and ½ cup of the Parmesan cheese. If made ahead, cover and refrigerate.

Bake, uncovered, in a 300° oven until top is crusty and sauce is bubbly (about 1 hour and 15 minutes). Cut in squares to serve. Makes 6 to 8 servings.

**White sauce.** In a 2-quart pan over medium heat, melt 4 tablespoons **butter** or margarine. Blend in ¼ cup **all-purpose flour,** ½ teaspoon **salt,** and ¼ teaspoon **ground nutmeg.** Cook, stirring, until bubbly. Remove pan from heat and gradually stir in 1½ cups **milk.** Return pan to heat and cook, stirring constantly, until sauce thickens and boils.

# Squares & Circles

## RAVIOLI, TORTELLINI, WON TON & OTHER STUFFED PILLOWS

One culinary idea that knows no borders is stuffed pillows—squares or circles of thinly rolled dough filled with a savory filling. Won ton and ravioli are probably the best-known examples. Indeed, there are as many Oriental recipes as Italian ones in this chapter. We've also included other versions of this pasta phenomenon from outside Italy and China.

Whenever we think of ravioli or tortellini, though, we think of the three gracious Italian women who not only shared with us their 50 years' cooking expertise and delicious recipes, but also taught us that the most important secret of making superb ravioli

and tortellini is to make them with a friend. With a friend to help, you can turn out several hundred stuffed pillows in just a few hours. Our Italian experts are used to working with as much as 5 pounds of flour at a time. But don't worry, you needn't start with such awesome quantities. We've scaled down their recipes to correspond to the dough recipes in the first chapter. The results are worth the work; once you've tasted homemade ravioli and tortellini, you'll never be satisfied with store bought versions again.

Stuffed pillows come in a variety of shapes. In the Oriental recipes, the same shape can

sometimes be boiled or deep-fried. We've included in this chapter our favorite pot sticker recipe from northern China and, of course, the popular won ton.

We haven't forgotten egg rolls, either. Surprisingly enough, we recommend buying the wrappers for won ton and egg rolls, though the eggless pasta dough (page 15) can be used instead. Oriental markets and many supermarkets carry won ton and egg roll wrappers. Many of our recipes make use of them. When you've become acquainted with these marvelous won ton wrappers, you'll probably want to invent fillings for your own deep-fried won ton appetizers.

## MAKING RAVIOLI

All-purpose pasta (page 8) makes excellent ravioli, and so do whole wheat pasta (page 8), spinach pasta (page 10), and semolina pasta (page 10).

Mix and knead the dough according to its recipe, just as you would for noodles. Aim for a dough that isn't sticky, but incorporates the maximum amount of liquid suggested in the recipe. This ensures a soft dough, and soft dough rolls out and seals more easily than firm dough—an important factor when making ravioli.

You can roll out the dough by hand or in a pasta machine. To shape and cut the dough, follow the directions for using one of the ravioli tools. These directions are general and can be applied to all the recipes in this chapter. First, though, a word of warning: there's a crucial difference between rolling out dough for ravioli and rolling out dough for noodles. You let the dough strips dry before cutting them into noodles, but you never let them dry when making ravioli because you want a moist dough that seals properly once it's filled.

**Ravioli rolling pin.** Using this tool is the fastest way to shape and

seal plump squares of dough and filling, though you still need a pasta machine or regular rolling pin to roll out the dough. Ravioli rolling pins come in various lengths and diameters. Some make 1-inch squares, others make larger ravioli. Our ravioli rolling pin, shown at right, is 24 inches long and makes 1-inch squares.

*If you roll out the dough by hand,* cut dough into 4 pieces and keep unrolled pieces covered. On a floured work surface, roll out 1 piece of dough about $\frac{1}{16}$ inch thick for bottom layer. With a knife or spatula, spread filling about $\frac{1}{4}$ inch thick over bottom layer; be sure filling extends

*(continued on page 36)*

# Two Ways to Cut Ravioli

## Ravioli rolling pin

**1.** Cut kneaded dough into 4 portions. With a standard rolling pin, roll out 2 of the portions to make 2 layers similar in size and shape. Spread filling on one layer; cover with second layer.

**2.** Slowly roll ravioli rolling pin across top, pressing down firmly to seal layers.

**3.** Run a floured, fluted pastry wheel along indentations to cut squares apart. Run pastry wheel along outer edge to seal any half-formed ravioli. Repeat with remaining dough.

## Ravioli frame & tray

**1.** Place dough strip on frame. Flour side of tray with convex circles and use it to press dough into hollows of frame. Remove tray.

**2.** Fill hollows with ravioli filling of your choice. Cover with another strip of dough, stretching it to cover frame completely.

**3.** Run a standard rolling pin over the top, pressing firmly so ravioli are sealed and cut. Trim off any excess dough. Tap one end of frame on work surface and invert to remove ravioli.

*...Making Ravioli (cont'd.)*

almost to edge of dough. For top layer, roll out another piece of dough to same size and thickness as bottom layer. Place on top of filled layer, stretching to cover bottom layer completely. Since it's hard to spread filling smoothly, without lumps or air pockets, it's a good idea to run a standard rolling pin very lightly over top layer of dough, just to even it out. Next, roll ravioli rolling pin slowly across top layer, pressing down firmly to seal dough layers and enclose filling in ravioli squares.

Finally, with a floured, fluted pastry wheel, cut filled squares apart along imprinted lines. Also run pastry wheel around outer edges to seal any half-formed ravioli (you can use these irregular ravioli for soup). With a spatula, transfer ravioli to a floured cooky sheet. Repeat entire procedure with remaining dough and filling. Cook or freeze according to recipe directions.

*If you roll out the dough with a pasta machine,* the steps for using a ravioli rolling pin are slightly different. First, cut dough into 4 pieces. Keeping unrolled pieces covered, work with 1 piece at a time. Roll out a strip to the third from the last setting. Do not let rolled strip dry. Immediately spread filling, about ¼ inch thick, over half the length of strip. Fold unfilled half back over filled portion. Even out filling by

lightly rolling a standard rolling pin across top. Then, with ravioli rolling pin, start rolling from widest side. Roll slowly, pressing firmly.

With a floured, fluted pastry wheel, cut filled squares apart along imprinted lines. Also run pastry wheel around outer edges to seal any half-formed ravioli (you can use these irregular ravioli for soup). With a spatula, transfer ravioli to a floured cooky sheet. Repeat entire procedure with remaining dough and filling. Cook or freeze according to recipe directions.

**Ravioli frame.** This ravioli tool (pictured on page 35) has two metal parts, a frame to shape the ravioli and a tray with indentations to press the dough into the frame. Some ravioli frames come with a small rolling pin, but a standard rolling pin works just as well. The frame and tray we used for testing measured 4 inches by 12 inches and made 12 ravioli, each about 1½ inches square. You can buy frames for larger or smaller ravioli, or larger frames to shape more ravioli. Roll dough strips to a size that fits your ravioli frame.

*If you roll out the dough by hand,* cut dough into 4 pieces. Keeping unrolled pieces covered, roll out 1 piece at a time on a floured work surface. Aim for a strip approximately 8 inches by 24 inches, so you can cut it into 4 strips, each 4 by 12 inches. Do not let rolled strip dry.

*If you roll out the dough in a pasta machine,* cut dough into 4 pieces. Keeping unrolled pieces covered, roll out 1 piece at a time. Stop rolling at the third to the last setting. (Each rolled dough strip should be at least 48 inches long.) Don't let rolled strip dry; cut it into 4 pieces, each 12 inches long.

When you're ready to use frame, flour it; then set one 12-inch strip on top. Flour side of tray that has convex circles and, with tray, press dough into hollows of frame. Remove tray. Place approximately 1 tablespoon of filling in each indentation. Cover with another strip of dough, stretching dough to cover tray completely. Pressing firmly, run

a standard rolling pin over top strip so frame seals and cuts ravioli squares. Gather up any dough scraps and cover them to be rolled out with remaining dough. To remove ravioli from frame, tap one end of frame on work surface and invert. With a spatula, transfer ravioli to a floured cooky sheet. Repeat entire procedure with remaining dough and filling. Cook or freeze according to recipe directions.

**Ravioli stamp.** Basically a cooky cutter for pasta, this tool comes in a variety of both round and square sizes. You can't substitute a cooky cutter for a ravioli stamp, though, because an ordinary cooky cutter won't seal dough as it cuts.

*If you roll out the dough by hand,* cut dough into 4 pieces. Keep unrolled pieces covered. On a floured work surface, roll out 1 piece about 1/16 inch thick for bottom layer. Do not let rolled strips dry. With a ravioli stamp, lightly mark off dough into as many squares or circles as possible. Place a small mound of filling on each square or circle. For top layer, roll out another piece of dough to same size and thickness as bottom layer. Place on top of filled layer, stretching it to cover bottom layer completely. Carefully press stamp into top layer to seal and cut ravioli. With a spatula, transfer ravioli to a floured cooky sheet. Gather up any dough scraps and cover them to be rolled out later. Repeat entire procedure with remaining dough and filling. Cook or freeze according to recipe directions.

*If you use a pasta machine,* cut dough into 4 pieces. Keeping unrolled pieces covered, work with 1 piece at a time. Roll out each strip to the third from the last setting. Do not let rolled strip dry. With a ravioli stamp, lightly mark off half the length of dough strip into as many squares or circles as possible. Place a small mound of filling on each square or circle. Fold other half of dough strip back over filled half. Carefully press stamp into top dough layer to seal and cut ravioli. With a spatula, transfer ravioli to a floured cooky sheet. Gather up any dough scraps and cover them to be rolled out later. Repeat entire procedure with remaining dough and filling. Cook or freeze according to recipe directions.

**Fluted pastry wheel.** Prepare dough exactly as you would for ravioli stamp, but use pastry wheel to mark off squares on bottom layer. Place a small mound of filling on each square, then cover with layer of rolled-out dough. Using floured pastry wheel, seal and cut ravioli. These ravioli won't be sealed as tightly as they would be with other tools, so expect a few ravioli to open during cooking.

## RAVIOLI IN BROTH

Ravioli in broth seems like the sort of time-consuming dish only a loving Italian *nonna* (grandmother) would prepare. Actually, it's a make-ahead dish that you can assemble at a moment's notice to delight an unexpected guest. Just prepare and freeze these light, chicken-and-ricotta-filled ravioli. At a later date, you can cook as many as you need and serve them in hot chicken broth. What could be easier? Figure on 8 to 12 ravioli for each bowl of broth.

**1 small package (3 oz.) cream cheese**
**3 egg yolks**
**1 cup ricotta cheese**
**¾ cup grated Parmesan cheese**
**⅓ cup minced, cooked chicken**
**¼ teaspoon salt**
**⅛ teaspoon ground nutmeg**
**Dash of white pepper**
**1 recipe all-purpose pasta (page 8)**
**Boiling salted water**
**Hot chicken broth (1½ cups per serving)**
**Grated Parmesan cheese**

To make filling, place cream cheese and egg yolks in a medium-size bowl and beat until smooth. Stir in ricotta, Parmesan, chicken, salt, nutmeg, and pepper until well mixed.

Follow directions on pages 34–36 for rolling out pasta dough and filling ravioli. Cook according to

directions that follow. Or transfer to floured cooky sheets and freeze until firm, then transfer to plastic bag for longer storage in freezer. Makes about 200 ravioli.

Figuring on 8 to 12 ravioli per serving, drop desired amount of freshly made or frozen ravioli into a large kettle of boiling salted water. When water returns to a boil, cook, stirring occasionally, until tender (8 to 10 minutes); then drain. Place 8 to 12 ravioli in each soup bowl. Ladle 1½ cups hot chicken broth over each serving. Sprinkle lightly with cheese before serving.

## ANOLINI IN BROTH

A specialty of Parma and Piacenza in the Italian province of Emilia-Romagna, these cheese-filled, round ravioli (anolini) are usually served in rich broth as a soup.

**1 egg**
**1 cup ricotta cheese**
**2 cups (8 oz.) shredded jack cheese**
**¼ cup *each* grated Parmesan cheese and fine dry bread crumbs**
**⅓ cup minced cooked ham**
**⅛ teaspoon ground nutmeg**
**1 recipe all-purpose pasta (page 8)**
**Boiling salted water**
**9 to 12 cups hot chicken broth or beef broth**
**Grated Parmesan cheese**

To make filling, beat egg in a medium-size bowl. Add ricotta, jack cheese, Parmesan, bread crumbs, ham, and nutmeg; mix well.

Roll out pasta in 4 strips (or by hand into 2 large squares), each about 1/16 inch thick. Drop filling by teaspoonfuls, about 1¾ inches apart, onto pasta. Cover pasta with another strip or sheet of pasta, and press down to seal dough between mounds of filling and along edges. Cut into anolini with a 1¾-inch round ravioli stamp or inverted glass. Place on floured cooky sheets. Cook according to directions that follow. Or freeze on cooky sheets until firm,

then transfer to plastic bags for longer storage in freezer.

To cook, drop freshly made or frozen anolini into a large kettle of boiling salted water. When water returns to a boil, cook, stirring occasionally, until tender (10 to 12 minutes); then drain. Place 6 to 8 anolini in each soup bowl. Ladle 1½ cups hot broth over each serving. Serve with Parmesan cheese. Makes 4 dozen anolini or 6 to 8 servings.

## OLD-FASHIONED RAVIOLI

You can't buy ravioli as good as these—not in any restaurant, and certainly not packaged commercially. Old-fashioned, meat-filled ravioli with meat sauce require the highest quality ingredients and take time—but the results are sublime.

We suggest pacing the preparation over several days, so the procedure won't seem so overwhelming. Mix the filling one day, but stop before the cheese and eggs are added and refrigerate it. The next day, mix in the cheese and eggs; fill the ravioli, and freeze them. You can make the sauce on another day and freeze it until you need it.

Another way to lessen the task is to invite a friend for a morning of ravioli-making and turn your kitchen into a ravioli factory. With a friend to help, you can make enough ravioli and sauce for several meals.

### Filling

**⅔ pound pork chops, cut ½ inch thick**
**½ pound boneless beef chuck, cut ½ inch thick**
**1 tablespoon olive oil**
**2 cloves garlic**
**3 sprigs parsley**
**¼ teaspoon *each* dry rosemary, thyme leaves, and salt**
**Dash of pepper**
**1 large bunch spinach or 1 package (10 or 12 oz.) frozen chopped spinach**
**2 tablespoons butter**
**1 or 2 eggs**
**2 tablespoons grated Romano or Parmesan cheese**

*(Continued on page 39)*

## Sauce

**1 pound ground chuck**
**2 tablespoons olive oil**
**1 large onion, finely chopped**
**4 cloves garlic, minced or pressed**
**½ bunch parsley, finely chopped**
**1 teaspoon dry basil**
**½ teaspoon *each* dry rosemary,**
**thyme leaves, and pepper**
**1 teaspoon salt**
**1 can (15 oz.) tomato purée**
**1 large can (1 lb. 12 oz.) tomatoes**
**1 cup water**

## Dough

**1 recipe all-purpose pasta**
**(page 8)**

**Boiling salted water**

## Topping

**Grated Romano or Parmesan**
**cheese**

To prepare filling, cut pork from bones (reserve bones for sauce). Trim excess fat and any gristle from pork and beef. Cut meat into 2-inch squares. Heat oil in a wide frying pan over medium-high heat. Add meat and cook until browned on both sides. Peel whole garlic and add to meat along with parsley, rosemary, thyme, salt, and pepper. Reduce heat to low and cook, uncovered, stirring occasionally, until pork is no longer pink when slashed (about 10 minutes).

While meat is cooking, cook fresh spinach in ½ inch of boiling water for 5 minutes (cook frozen spinach according to package directions); drain. When cool enough to handle, press spinach with your hands to remove as much water as possible. Melt butter in a frying pan over medium heat. Add spinach and cook, stirring, for 3 minutes.

Using a food processor or the finest blade of a meat grinder, very

finely chop meat mixture. Finely chop spinach as well, but do not purée. Combine meat and spinach. (At this point you may cover and refrigerate until next day; let mixture come to room temperature before continuing.) Beat 1 egg and stir into meat mixture along with cheese. If mixture seems stiff, beat another egg and stir into mixture. Set aside.

To prepare sauce, cook meat in 1 tablespoon of the oil in a wide frying pan over medium-high heat until crumbly and browned. Transfer meat to a Dutch oven. Add the remaining 1 tablespoon oil to frying pan. Add onion, garlic, and bones (reserved when making the filling). Cook, stirring, until onion is limp. Add parsley, basil, rosemary, thyme, pepper, and salt; cook for 1 minute. Spoon onion mixture over meat. Add tomato purée to meat. Strain tomato liquid to remove seeds, then add liquid to meat. Slit tomatoes, squeeze out seeds, chop, and add to meat. Stir in water. Bring sauce to a boil, then cover, reduce heat, and simmer, stirring occasionally, for 2 hours or until sauce is thickened. Set aside. Or, if made ahead, cool, cover, and refrigerate (or freeze for longer storage).

Follow directions on pages 34–36 for rolling out pasta dough and filling ravioli. Cook according to directions that follow. Or transfer to floured cooky sheets and freeze until firm, then transfer to plastic bags for longer storage in freezer.

To cook, drop freshly made or frozen ravioli into a large kettle of boiling salted water and boil gently, stirring occasionally, until tender (10 to 12 minutes); then drain. While ravioli are cooking, heat sauce. Allow ¾ to 1 cup sauce for every 50 ravioli. Ladle ravioli into a serving bowl and spoon sauce over top. Sprinkle with Romano cheese before serving. Makes about 200 1-inch ravioli.

## PIEDMONT-STYLE RAVIOLI

These large ravioli are sometimes called *agnolotti* or "fat little lambs." The delicious filling combines ground chicken, spinach, and a hint of nutmeg. The sauce is made from the liquid in which the chicken was cooked.

**2 tablespoons butter or margarine**
**1½ pounds chicken breasts,**
**boned, skinned, and cut into**
**1-inch squares**
**1 medium-size onion, chopped**
**1 clove garlic, minced or pressed**
**½ teaspoon salt**
**⅛ teaspoon dry rosemary**
**Dash of white pepper**
**1 cup *each* tomato juice and dry**
**white wine**
**1 cup packed fresh spinach leaves**
**1 egg, lightly beaten**
**¼ cup grated Parmesan cheese**
**¼ cup finely chopped prosciutto**
**or boiled ham**
**¼ teaspoon ground nutmeg**
**1 recipe all-purpose pasta**
**(page 8)**
**Boiling salted water**
**2 tablespoons firm butter or**
**margarine, cut in small pieces**
**Grated Parmesan cheese**

In a wide frying pan over medium-high heat, melt butter and brown chicken breasts well on all sides. Add onion and garlic and cook until onion is limp. Sprinkle with salt, rosemary, and pepper; add tomato juice and wine. Bring to a boil; then cover, reduce heat, and simmer until chicken is tender (about 20 minutes). Reserve liquid in pan for sauce. Using a food processor or finest blade of a meat grinder, very finely chop chicken and uncooked spinach. Combine with egg, Parmesan, prosciutto, and nutmeg; mix well.

Roll out pasta by machine into 4 strips (or by hand into 2 large squares) each about $\frac{1}{16}$ inch thick. Drop filling by teaspoonfuls, about 1¾ inches apart, onto freshly rolled pasta (do not let pasta dry before filling). Cover pasta with another strip or sheet of pasta, and press down between mounds of filling, and at edges, to seal. Cut into 1¾-inch squares. With a spatula, lift ravioli from board. Cook according to directions that follow. Or transfer to floured cooky sheets and freeze until firm, then transfer to plastic bags for longer storage in freezer.

*(Continued on next page)*

Place ravioli in boiling salted water. Return to a boil and cook, stirring frequently, until tender (10 to 12 minutes). Drain well.

While pasta is cooking, prepare sauce. Reheat reserved cooking liquid (from chicken). Stirring occasionally, bring to a boil. Cook for a few minutes until liquid is reduced and thickened slightly. Swirl in pieces of firm butter until melted. Transfer pasta onto warm plates; spoon a little sauce over each portion and sprinkle with Parmesan. Makes 5 dozen ravioli or 8 servings.

---

# BIG OR LITTLE RAVIOLI WITH ITALIAN GRAVY

If you've thought of making ravioli but felt it was too big a job, this short-cut method may appeal to you. The trick is to use purchased won ton skins or egg roll wrappers instead of homemade dough.

An old Italian cook may say this is not a true ravioli, but the results make fine eating, even though the flavor of the Oriental wrappers is a little more bland than dough made with fresh eggs. This quick wrap is also a good idea if you want to try out different ravioli fillings, but don't want to commit your time to the pasta-making process.

Use won ton skins to make super-size ravioli; use egg roll wrappers to cut into regular-size ravioli. Both can be found in the refrigerator or freezer case of many supermarkets.

### Filling

**1¼ pounds chicken breasts or 1 set (about ½ lb.) calf's brains**
**2 packages (10 or 12 oz. *each*) frozen chopped spinach**
**1 package (12 oz.) frozen chopped Swiss chard**
**2 cups (6 oz.) grated Parmesan cheese**
**½ cup finely chopped parsley**
**1 tablespoon marjoram leaves**
**1 teaspoon salt**
**½ teaspoon *each* garlic salt, pepper, and ground allspice**
**6 eggs**
**6 tablespoons olive oil or salad oil**

### Wrappers

**2 packages (1 lb. *each*) egg roll wrappers or 1 package (1 lb.) won ton skins**

### Italian gravy

**2½ ounces dried Italian mushrooms**
**4 cups warm water**
**3 tablespoons olive oil or salad oil**
**3-pound piece lean boneless chuck roast**
**3 large onions, finely chopped**
**1 cup finely chopped parsley**
**1 tablespoon dry rosemary**
**1½ teaspoons marjoram leaves**
**3 cloves garlic, minced or pressed**
**1 bay leaf**
**3 cans (6 oz. *each*) tomato paste**
**¾ cup dry white wine**
**5 cups water**
**Salt and pepper to taste**

**Boiling salted water**

### Topping

**About 2 cups (6 oz.) grated Parmesan cheese**

To make filling, simmer chicken breasts in water to cover for 20 minutes or until tender. When cool enough to handle, discard skin and bones. Using a food processor or finest blade of a meat grinder, very finely chop chicken. (Or soak calf's brains in cold water for 30 minutes, then remove thin membrane. Poach brains in gently boiling water for 15 minutes or until firm throughout, then plunge into cold water to cool quickly. Drain well and grind or chop in food processor.)

Cook spinach and Swiss chard according to package directions; drain well. With your hands, press out as much water as possible. Finely chop greens and combine with meat, cheese, parsley, marjoram, salt, garlic salt, pepper, and allspice. Cover and refrigerate for as long as 24 hours, if desired. When ready to prepare ravioli, beat eggs with oil. Add to meat mixture and mix well.

**To fill egg roll wrappers,** place 1 skin on a piece of wax paper and spread about 3 tablespoons filling evenly to edges; place another wrap-

per on top. With a ruler or straight edge, indent dough to mark off 16 equal squares; with a pastry wheel, run along indentations and around edges, through all layers, to seal. Because egg roll wrappers are not as pliable as fresh pasta, it's necessary to press down very firmly with pastry wheel to seal edges. Remove and discard dough scraps. Set aside ravioli on paper. Repeat with remaining wrappers and filling.

**To fill won ton skins,** place 1 skin on wax paper and evenly spread 1 tablespoon filling to edges. Cover with another skin and, pressing down firmly, run a pastry wheel just inside edges to seal. Remove dough scraps. Repeat with remaining skins and filling.

This much can be done ahead; cover and refrigerate filled ravioli until next day or wrap well and freeze for longer storage.

To make gravy, cover mushrooms with warm water; let stand for at least 30 minutes. Heat oil in a heavy 5-quart kettle over medium-high heat; add roast and brown very well on all sides. Lift out meat and set aside.

Add onions to pan drippings and cook over medium heat until limp. Stir in parsley, rosemary, marjoram, garlic, bay leaf, tomato paste, wine, and the 5 cups water. Squeeze water from mushrooms (reserve water) and finely chop. Add mushrooms to kettle along with their water (discard any residue at bottom of water).

Return roast to kettle and season to taste with salt and pepper. Cover, reduce heat, and simmer until meat is very tender when pierced (about 1½ hours). Remove meat. If you prefer a thicker gravy, continue to cook gravy, uncovered, until it reaches desired thickness. Serve gravy hot. Or cool, cover, and refrigerate for as long as 2 days (freeze for longer storage); then reheat when needed. Slice meat. Serve along with the ravioli or cover and chill meat with some gravy for another meal.

To cook ravioli, drop freshly made, chilled, or frozen ravioli into a large kettle of boiling salted water. When water returns to a boil, cook gently, uncovered, just until wrappers are tender to bite (6 to 8 minutes). Drain carefully and thoroughly.

To serve, spoon a small amount of hot Italian gravy onto a large, rimmed serving platter, top with some of the ravioli, then add more gravy and sprinkle with Parmesan cheese. Repeat layers. Pass additional cheese at the table. Makes 8 to 10 servings.

## GERMAN RAVIOLI WITH ONION SAUCE

Served with buttery sautéed onions, these envelopes of pasta filled with pork and beef are a popular supper dish in the Black Forest region of Germany.

### Filling

1 pound lean ground pork
½ pound lean ground beef
1 medium-size onion, finely
    chopped
1 teaspoon salt
¼ teaspoon *each* thyme leaves
    and marjoram leaves
⅛ teaspoon *each* ground nutmeg
    and white pepper
½ cup lightly packed chopped
    parsley
¼ cup soft bread crumbs
1 egg

### Dough

1 recipe all-purpose pasta
    (page 8)

### Onion sauce

4 medium-size onions, thinly
    sliced
¼ cup butter or margarine
½ teaspoon salt
⅛ teaspoon ground nutmeg
⅓ cup dry white wine

    Boiling salted water

### Garnish

    Chopped parsley
    Tomato slices

To make filling, crumble pork and beef in a wide frying pan over medium-high heat and cook, stirring, until lightly browned. Add onion and continue cooking until onion is limp. Remove from heat; spoon off excess fat. Mix in salt, thyme, marjo-

ram, nutmeg, pepper, parsley, and bread crumbs. Beat egg; stir into meat mixture. Cool.

Roll out pasta by machine into 4 strips (or by hand into 2 large squares), each about ¹⁄₁₆ inch thick. Cut into 4 by 5-inch rectangles. You should have about 2 dozen rectangles.

Place about 2 tablespoons filling on one half of each rectangle; fold dough in half to make 2½ by 4-inch rectangles. Press edges together firmly to seal. Cook according to directions that follow. Or transfer to floured cooky sheets and freeze until firm, then transfer to plastic bags for longer storage in freezer.

To make sauce, cook onions in butter in a wide frying pan over medium-low heat, stirring frequently, until tender and golden brown (20 to 25 minutes). Add salt, nutmeg, and wine; increase heat and cook, stirring, until liquid is reduced by one-half.

To cook pasta, drop 12 ravioli at a time into a large kettle of boiling salted water. When water returns to a boil, cook pasta until tender (12 to 15 minutes). Remove pasta with a slotted spoon, drain well, and place on a large, rimmed serving platter. Keep warm while you cook remainder of ravioli.

To serve, spoon onion sauce over pasta. Sprinkle with parsley; garnish with tomato slices. Makes 6 to 8 servings.

## PANSOTTI WITH WALNUT SAUCE

Here are triangular ravioli enjoyed along the sunny coast of Italy, south of Genoa, in such seaside resorts as Portofino and Rapallo. In Italian, these ravioli are called *pansotti,* which could be translated as "pot-bellied," referring (one hopes) to the plumpness of each little pasta pillow filled with spinach, eggs, and cheese. The perfect sauce for pansotti is not cooked; it's made with ground, toasted walnuts and served at room temperature over the steaming pasta.

½ cup finely chopped, well
    drained, cooked spinach
1 cup ricotta cheese
½ cup grated Parmesan cheese
3 hard-cooked eggs, finely
    chopped
¼ cup fine dry bread crumbs
¼ teaspoon ground nutmeg
1 recipe all-purpose pasta
    (page 8).
1½ cups coarsely chopped
    walnuts
1 cup whipping cream
1 small clove garlic, minced or
    pressed
¼ teaspoon salt
⅛ teaspoon white pepper
    Boiling salted water
    Sweet butter
    Grated Parmesan cheese

To make filling, mix spinach, ricotta, Parmesan, eggs, bread crumbs, and nutmeg.

*(Continued on next page)*

Roll out pasta into 4 strips (or by hand into 2 large squares), each about $\frac{1}{16}$ inch thick. Cut into 2½-inch squares. Place a heaping teaspoon of filling on half of each square; fold each square in half to make a triangle. Moistening edges, if necessary, press edges firmly together to seal. Cook according to directions that follow. Or transfer to floured cooky sheets and freeze until firm, then transfer to plastic bags for longer storage in freezer.

To make sauce, spread walnuts in a shallow baking pan. Bake in a 350° oven until browned (10 to 12 minutes); cool slightly. Place in blender or food processor with cream, garlic, salt, and pepper; whirl or process until smooth. If made ahead, refrigerate; let come to room temperature before serving.

To cook, drop freshly made or frozen pansotti in a large kettle of boiling salted water. Return to a boil and cook until tender (10 to 12 minutes). Drain well.

To serve, mix pansotti with sweet butter to taste. Top with walnut sauce (at room temperature); sprinkle with Parmesan cheese. Makes 5 dozen pansotti or 6 to 8 servings.

# CHICKEN LIVER KREPLACH

Kreplach, the Jewish won ton, can be cooked and served in broth; or it can be boiled, then fried until golden.

It's slightly unorthodox, but for maximum flavor, try frying boiled kreplach in butter and serving it with sour cream or sautéed onion rings.

**2 tablespoons rendered chicken fat or salad oil**
**½ small onion, finely chopped**
**¼ pound mushrooms, sliced**
**½ pound chicken livers, cut in half**
**2 tablespoons chopped parsley**
**¼ teaspoon *each* thyme leaves and salt**
 **Dash of white pepper**
**1 recipe all-purpose pasta (page 8)**
 **Boiling salted water**
 **Hot chicken broth (1 cup per serving)**

Place chicken fat in a wide frying pan over medium-high heat. Add onion and mushrooms and cook for 3 minutes. Add chicken livers, parsley, thyme, salt, and pepper; reduce heat to medium and cook, stirring occasionally, until livers are just firm but slightly pink in center (about 10 minutes). In a food processor or blender, purée chicken liver mixture. Cool.

Roll out pasta by machine into 4 strips (or by hand into 2 large squares), each about $\frac{1}{16}$ inch thick. Cut in 2-inch squares. Place ½ teaspoon filling in center of each square; fold each square in half diagonally to make a triangle. Moistening edges, if necessary, press firmly together to seal. Cook according to directions that follow. Or transfer to floured cooky sheets and freeze until firm, then transfer to plastic bags for longer storage in freezer. Makes about 9 dozen kreplach.

Figuring on 8 kreplach per serving, drop freshly made or frozen kreplach into a large kettle of boiling salted water. When water returns to a boil, cook, stirring occasionally, until tender (about 10 minutes); then drain. Place 8 kreplach in each serving bowl. Ladle 1 cup hot chicken broth over each serving.

# MONTI IN BROTH

*(Pictured on page 38)*

For soups, Armenian cooks make a filled pasta called *monti* that is uniquely different from Italian ravioli or the stuffed pasta specialties of other countries.

You fold squares of dough in a boatlike shape around a filling of ground lamb mildly seasoned with onion and lots of fresh parsley. Unlike most ravioli, monti are not cooked in liquid; they're baked crusty and brown, then served in beef broth with a refreshing yogurt topping.

If you wish, you can mix the dough for monti in a food processor, but for rolling out the tender dough, a rolling pin works better than a pasta machine. And it's helpful to freeze monti after baking—then you can remove only as many at a time as you need to heat and serve.

**Dough**
 **1 egg**
 **⅓ cup water**
 **⅛ teaspoon salt**
 **2 tablespoons melted butter or margarine**
 **1½ cups plus 2 tablespoons all-purpose flour**

**Filling**
 **½ pound lean ground lamb**
 **1 small onion, minced**
 **¼ cup finely chopped parsley**
 **½ teaspoon salt**
 **⅛ teaspoon pepper**
 **2 tablespoons butter or margarine**

**Yogurt sauce**
 **1 cup unflavored yogurt**
 **1 small clove garlic, minced or pressed**
 **¼ teaspoon salt**
 **¼ cup finely chopped parsley**

**Soup**
 **3 cans (14 oz. *each*) beef broth**
 **2 tablespoons catsup**
 **¼ teaspoon liquid hot pepper seasoning**

In a bowl or food processor, combine egg, water, salt, and butter. Add flour and stir or process until mixture forms a ball. Turn dough out on a lightly floured board and knead until dough is smooth and elastic (about 8 minutes, or 1 minute if mixed in processor). Cover dough and let rest for 30 minutes.

To make filling, combine lamb, onion, parsley, salt, and pepper. Mix until well blended. Melt butter in a 10 by 15-inch baking pan.

On a lightly floured board, roll out half the dough at a time to form a 9-inch square about ⅛ inch thick. Cut dough into 1½-inch squares. Repeat with other half of dough. You should get about 36 squares from each half.

Keeping dough and filled monti covered with plastic wrap as you work, place ½ teaspoon of filling on each square. Fold up 2 sides of each square and pinch ends together into a boat shape. As each monti is shaped, place it, filling side up, in buttered pan.

Bake monti in a 375° oven until browned (35 to 40 minutes). If made ahead, cool, cover, and refrigerate for as long as 2 days. Or transfer to cooky sheets and freeze until firm, then transfer to plastic bags for longer storage in freezer.

To make yogurt sauce, combine yogurt, garlic, salt, and parsley in a bowl. Cover and refrigerate for at least 1 hour.

To make soup, combine broth, catsup, and hot pepper seasoning in a large kettle. Heat to boiling. Add fresh or frozen baked monti to broth, reduce heat, and simmer until they are heated through (5 to 10 minutes). Serve in wide soup bowls. Pass yogurt sauce at the table. Makes 6 to 8 servings.

## PELMENI

The Russian version of ravioli features a filling of spiced ground beef. Since ordinary ground beef is too coarse for pelmeni, the meat should be ground a second time if you will not be using a food processor.

With its touch of cinnamon, pelmeni is delicious served with sour cream and pickeled beets. For variety, you could also serve pelmeni in beef broth.

**¾ pound lean ground beef**
**1 small onion, finely chopped**
**1 tablespoon salad oil**
**¼ teaspoon *each* salt and ground cinnamon**
**⅛ teaspoon pepper**
**2 eggs**
**1 recipe all-purpose pasta (page 8)**
**Boiling salted water**
**About 4 tablespoons butter or margarine**
**Sour cream**
**Pickled beets**

In a wide frying pan over medium-high heat, cook meat and onion in salad oil until meat is crumbly and browned. Add salt, cinnamon, and pepper; cook for 2 minutes. For a fine-grained filling, finely chop meat mixture in a food processor. Add eggs and process until well mixed. Cool.

Roll out pasta by machine into 4 strips (or by hand into 2 large squares), each about ¹⁄₁₆ inch thick. Cut in 2-inch circles. Place 1 teaspoon filling in center of each circle; fold each circle in half to make a half moon. Moistening edges, press edges firmly together to seal. Cook according to directions that follow. Or transfer to floured cooky sheets and freeze until firm; then transfer to plastic bags for longer storage in freezer.

Drop freshly made or frozen pelmeni into a large kettle of boiling salted water. When water returns to a boil, cook pasta gently, stirring occasionally, until tender (10 to 12 minutes); then drain.

Melt 2 tablespoons of the butter in a wide frying pan over medium heat. Place a single layer of pelmeni in pan and cook until lightly browned (about 3 minutes on each side). Remove from pan and keep warm while you brown remaining pelmeni, adding butter as needed to keep pasta from sticking. Serve with a topping of sour cream and garnish with pickled beets. Makes about 8 dozen pelmeni or 6 to 8 main-dish servings.

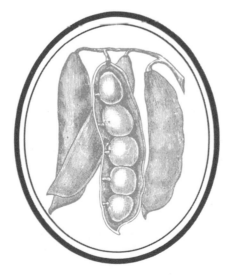

## MAKING TORTELLINI

Once upon a time the goddess Venus stayed at a Bolognese inn. Overwhelmed with curiosity, the innkeeper couldn't resist peeking at her through a keyhole. Catching a glimpse of her bellybutton, he immediately rushed out to celebrate the vision in the artistic medium he knew best—not clay, not marble, but pasta. He ran to his kitchen and created what we know as tortellini (literally, "little twists").

If little else, this Boccaccio-type tale reflects the love the citizens of Bologna have for one of their most famous dishes.

To make perfect little bellybutton-shaped tortellini, use all-purpose pasta (page 8), or semolina pasta (page 10). At the risk of insulting the goddess of love, you could also make tortellini out of whole wheat pasta (page 8), spinach pasta (page 10), or the orange or rosy pasta (page 10).

The following directions tell how to fill and fold tortellini. The directions are followed by two recipes, each providing a tortellini filling and complementary sauce. You might want to borrow a ravioli or cappelletti filling, or invent your own from bits of leftover meat, cheese, and egg (to bind). You'll need approximately 1½ cups filling for each batch of dough made with 2 cups flour.

Mix dough according to the pasta recipe you choose. Try to incorporate the maximum amount of water the recipe suggests, but do not let the dough become sticky. Like ravioli, tortellini seals better if the dough is soft rather than firm.

After kneading the dough, you can roll it out by hand or with a pasta machine. Work with one-fourth of the dough at a time (do not let it dry). Keep the unrolled portion covered.

If rolling by hand, roll dough ¹⁄₁₆ inch thick, as for lasagne. If rolling with a pasta machine, roll dough to the third from the last setting.

Use a glass or round cooky cutter

2 to 3 inches in diameter to cut out as many circles from the rolled dough as possible. Gather up any dough scraps and cover them to be rolled out with remaining dough.

Use the filling of your choice and, follow the illustrations below to fill

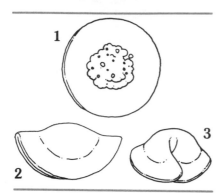

and shape tortellini. 1. Place ½ teaspoon filling in middle of each circle. 2. Fold circle in half; moistening edges, if necessary, press edges together to seal. 3. Draw ends together so they overlap. Press to seal (moisten, if necessary). Repeat this procedure with remaining dough and filling.

Place tortellini on floured cooky sheets and cook tortellini or freeze according to recipe directions.

Another version of tortellini looks more like rings. To make ringlike tortellini, follow steps 1 and 2 above, then roll the filled half-circle to make a tube of dough. Wrap the tube around your index finger, overlapping the ends. Press the ends together to seal.

## TORTELLINI SUPREME

Indulge yourself in a trip to an Italian market or delicatessen to pick up the three main ingredients for tortellini supreme. The filling includes two distinctive Italian meats: prosciutto (Italy's favorite cured ham) and mortadella (Bologna's famous sausage, the superior original of American bologna). The sauce calls for asiago cheese, but for sharper flavor you could substitute Romano or Parmesan cheese.

### Filling

  **½ pound prosciutto**
  **2 thin slices mortadella (about 1 oz. total)**
  **¼ cup grated Parmesan cheese**
  **⅛ teaspoon ground nutmeg**
  **2 egg yolks**

  **1 recipe all-purpose pasta (page 8)**

### Sauce

  **½ cup (¼ lb.) butter**
  **2 tablespoons all-purpose flour**
  **2 cups whipping cream**
  **¼ teaspoon ground nutmeg**
  **1 cup (3 oz.) grated asiago cheese**

    **Boiling salted water**

To make filling, use a food processor or finest blade of a meat grinder to very finely chop prosciutto and mortadella. Combine meats with Parmesan, nutmeg, and egg yolks; mix well.

Follow directions on page 43 for rolling out pasta dough and filling tortellini. Cook according to directions that follow. Or transfer to floured cooky sheets and freeze until firm, then transfer to plastic bags for longer storage in freezer.

To make sauce, melt butter in a 2-quart pan over medium heat. Add flour and cook until bubbly. Stir in cream and nutmeg and cook, stirring, until smooth and thickened. Stir in asiago and cook until cheese melts. If made ahead, cool, cover, and refrigerate; reheat over hot water, stirring until smooth.

To cook pasta, drop freshly made or frozen tortellini into a large kettle of boiling salted water. When water returns to a boil, cook pasta gently, stirring occasionally, until tender (8 to 10 minutes); then drain. Place tortellini on individual plates. Pour sauce over each serving. Makes about 10 dozen tortellini or 6 to 8 main course servings.

## CHEESE-FILLED TORTELLINI

Mint and basil add a spring-fresh flavor to the two-cheese filling. Instead of a tomato sauce that might overwhelm the delicate filling, a simple sauce of sautéed onions complements the tortellini. For a triple cheese treat, you could serve these with the tortellini supreme sauce.

### Filling

  **1 cup ricotta cheese**
  **½ cup grated Romano cheese**
  **2 teaspoons minced fresh mint or 1 teaspoon dry mint**
  **2 teaspoons minced fresh basil leaves or 1 teaspoon dry basil**
  **½ teaspoon salt**
    **Dash of white pepper**
  **2 egg yolks**

  **1 recipe all-purpose pasta (page 8)**

### Onion sauce

  **5 tablespoons butter**
  **3 tablespoons olive oil**
  **2 large onions, coarsely chopped**
  **¼ teaspoon *each* salt and ground nutmeg**

    **Boiling salted water**
    **Grated Romano cheese**

To make filling, combine ricotta, Romano, mint, basil, salt, pepper, and egg yolks; mix well.

Follow directions on page 43 for rolling out pasta dough and filling tortellini. Cook according to directions that follow. Or transfer to floured cooky sheets and freeze until firm, then transfer to plastic bags for longer storage in freezer.

To make onion sauce, heat butter and oil in a wide frying pan over low heat. Add onions and cook, stirring occasionally, until very limp (about 20 minutes). Stir in salt and nutmeg. Keep warm.

To cook pasta, drop freshly made or frozen tortellini into a large kettle of boiling salted water. When water returns to a boil, cook pasta gently, stirring occasionally, until tender (8 to 10 minutes); then drain. Place half the tortellini in a shallow serving dish. Spoon half the onion sauce over tortellini. Repeat, using remainder of tortellini and onion sauce. Sprinkle lightly with Romano cheese before serving. Makes 6 to 8 servings.

# MAKING CAPPELLETTI

Cappelletti are "little hats." Our favorite version is a hat with double peaks that look like Mercury's wings. The story goes that a grateful cook created Mercury's hats to celebrate some good news he had received. (Mercury, you may remember, was the messenger of the Roman gods.) Other versions of cappelletti look like bishops' mitres or cardinals' hats.

To make cappelletti, mix, knead, and roll out the dough as you would for tortellini. Then, using the recipe for cappelletti with tomato-cream sauce on this page or one of the tortellini fillings at left, cut, fill, and shape the hats according to the directions that follow. Once you've filled and shaped the hats, place them on floured cooky sheets and cook or freeze according to directions in recipe for filling.

To shape Mercury's hats, follow the illustrations below. 1. With a

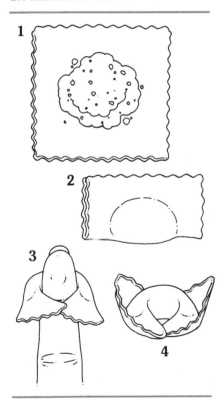

floured pastry wheel, cut rolled dough into 2 to 3-inch squares. Place about ½ teaspoon filling in

center of each square. 2. Fold each square in half to make a rectangle. Moistening edges, if necessary, press edges firmly together to seal. 3. Wrap rectangle around your index finger. Overlap the folded ends and press together to seal (moisten, if necessary). 4. Pull the two points up to make the hat's peaks. Repeat entire procedure with remaining dough and filling.

Follow the illustrations below to make bishops' mitres.

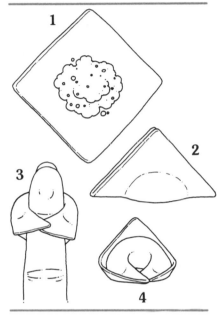

1. With a knife, cut rolled dough into 2 to 3-inch squares. Place about ½ teaspoon filling in center of each square. 2. Fold each square into a triangle. Moistening edges, if necessary, press edges firmly together to seal. 3. Wrap long side of triangle around your index finger. Overlap ends and press to seal (moisten, if necessary). 4. Pull pointy end of triangle back over plump part of dough to make the peak. Repeat entire procedure with remaining dough and filling.

Cardinals' hats are made with circles of dough, as shown in illustrations at top right.

1. With a small glass or round cooky cutter 2 to 3 inches in diameter, cut out as many circles from the rolled dough as possible. Place about ½ teaspoon filling in center of each circle. 2. Fold each circle in

half. Moistening edges, if necessary, press edges firmly together to seal. 3. Wrap folded side of half-circle around your index finger. Overlap ends and press to seal (moisten, if necessary). 4. Bend outer edge back to form the hat's round crown. Repeat entire procedure with remaining dough and filling.

# CAPPELLETTI WITH TOMATO-CREAM SAUCE

The hardest part of this recipe is deciding whether to fold the cappelletti into Mercury's hats, cardinals' hats, or bishops' mitres. The filling is easy to make, and the tomato-cream sauce is just a matter of cooking finely chopped vegetables and adding cream.

Both the cappelletti and the tomato-cream sauce can be made in advance. The brightly colored sauce is so attractive and tasty that you'll probably want to use it on other pastas as well.

To complement the cappelletti, serve a crisp salad—a variety of greens tossed with a simple oil and vinegar or oil and lemon dressing.

*(Continued on next page)*

## Filling

**1 cup ricotta cheese**
**½ cup grated Parmesan cheese**
**1 teaspoon grated onion**
**½ teaspoon salt**
**2 egg yolks**

**1 recipe all-purpose pasta (page
    8) or spinach pasta (page 10)**

## Tomato-cream sauce

**6 tablespoons butter**
**1 *each* small onion, celery stalk,
    and medium-size carrot, all
    finely chopped**
**1 can (about 1 lb.) tomatoes**
**1 teaspoon dry basil**
    **Dash *each* of salt and white
    pepper**
**¼ to ⅓ cup whipping cream**

    **Boiling salted water**
**1 cup (3 oz.) grated Parmesan
    cheese**

To make filling, combine ricotta, Parmesan, onion, salt, and egg yolks until well mixed.

Follow directions on page 45 for rolling out pasta dough and filling cappelletti. Cook according to directions that follow. Or transfer to floured cooky sheets and freeze until firm, then transfer to plastic bags for longer storage in freezer.

To make sauce, melt butter in a wide frying pan over medium-low heat. Add onion, celery, and carrot and cook until vegetables are soft but not browned (about 15 minutes). Stir in tomatoes and their liquid (crush tomatoes first with a spoon or process briefly in a food processor). Add basil, salt, and pepper. Cover and simmer, stirring occasionally, for 30 minutes.

Stir in enough cream so sauce has the consistency of gravy. If made ahead, cool, cover, and refrigerate. When needed, reheat over low heat, stirring frequently.

To cook pasta, drop freshly made or frozen cappelletti into a large kettle of boiling salted water. When water returns to a boil, cook pasta gently, stirring occasionally, until tender (8 to 10 minutes); then drain. Place cappelletti in a wide, shallow serving dish, pour over sauce, and sprinkle with some grated cheese.

Pass remainder of cheese at table. Makes about 10 dozen cappelletti or 6 to 8 main-dish servings.

## MAKING WON TON

If you were to name the most popular stuffed pasta in international cooking, it would be hard to choose between ravioli from the West and won ton from the Far East. Both of these stuffed pillows can be simmered in soups, sauced for dumplings, or fried for appetizers. And the range of fillings that go inside the pasta wrap is limitless.

From a cook's point of view, the striking difference between these two pastas is the starting point. Ravioli dough must be made from scratch; won ton wrappers can be purchased, ready to stuff. The wrappers (or skins) come fresh or frozen in 1-pound packages containing 60 to 70 squares.

If you wish to make your own skins, though, you can use the recipe for eggless pasta, page 15; it most closely resembles packaged won ton. Roll out the dough by hand to ¹⁄₁₆-inch thickness, or roll it out with a pasta machine and stop at the third from the last setting. Then cut pasta into 3-inch squares. One recipe yields about 40 won ton skins. Homemade won ton skins are best to use in soup or in recipes that call for cooking in liquid. But for deep-fried won ton, you will have a crispier crust if you use packaged skins.

There are several ways to fold won ton. For the prettiest and most traditional way, follow the illustration below. 1. Place a won ton skin

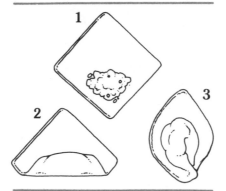

on your work surface. (Cover remaining skins with a damp towel to keep them pliable.) Mound 1 teaspoon filling in one corner. 2. Fold that corner over filling, and roll to tuck point under. Moisten the two side corners with water or beaten egg. 3. Bring side corners together, overlapping them slightly. Pinch together firmly to seal. Place filled won ton slightly apart on a baking sheet and cover while you fill the remaining skins.

A faster way to wrap won ton is to dot filling in center of the skin, pull the edges around filling, moisten with water or egg, and squeeze slightly to seal. Or you can fold the won ton skins in half diagonally to form triangles.

If made ahead, cover and refrigerate won ton for as long as 8 hours before cooking them. Or transfer to cooky sheets and freeze until firm, then transfer to plastic bags for longer storage in freezer. Fried won tons can be frozen, too, but after they are deep-fried.

## WON TON COOKIES

Wrap won ton skins around a sweet filling and the noodle squares become a delicious make-ahead dessert. This recipe fills 3 dozen won ton skins—half the amount that comes in a standard 1-pound package. You can double the filling if you wish to make a large batch of cookies, or use the remaining 3 dozen wrappers with one of the other won ton fillings found in this chapter.

**¼ cup sesame seeds**
**¼ cup firmly packed brown sugar**
**½ cup finely chopped pitted dates**
**1 tablespoon softened butter or
    margarine**
**½ package (1-lb. size) won ton
    skins**
**1 egg, lightly beaten**
    **Salad oil**
    **Powdered sugar**

In a heavy frying pan over medium heat, toast sesame seeds, shaking pan occasionally, until they turn golden and begin to pop (about 2 minutes); cool, then crush seeds coarsely. In a bowl, combine sesame seeds, brown sugar, dates, and butter.

Using 1 teaspoon filling for each won ton and moistening edges with egg to seal, fill and wrap won ton according to directions on page 46.

Into a deep pan, pour oil to a depth of about 1½ inches and heat to 350° on a deep-frying thermometer. Fry 4 to 6 won ton at a time for 1 minute or until golden. Remove with a slotted spoon and drain on paper towels. When completely cooled, sprinkle with powdered sugar. Store in an airtight container. Makes about 3 dozen cookies.

## FRIED WON TON

Won ton that are deep-fried make excellent appetizers. You can choose from several fillings and dipping sauces. Each filling is enough for a 1-pound package of won ton skins. If you want to make them ahead, deep-fry the won ton before freezing, then reheat in the oven.

**Shrimp, pork, or chorizo and beef filling (recipes follow)**
**1 package (1 lb.) won ton skins**
**1 egg, lightly beaten**
**Salad oil**
**Dipping sauces: chile sauce, tartar sauce, hot mustard, catsup, guacamole or frozen avocado dip (thawed)**

Prepare filling of your choice, then fill and wrap won ton according to directions on page 46. Use 1 teaspoon filling for each won ton and moisten edges with egg to seal.

Into a deep pan, pour oil to a depth of about 1½ inches and heat to 350° on a deep-frying thermometer. Fry 4 to 6 won ton at a time for 1 minute or until golden. Remove with a slotted spoon and drain on paper towels. Keep warm in a 200° oven until all are cooked. Serve with dipping sauce of your choice. Makes 5 to 6 dozen won ton.

If made ahead, cool fried won ton, then freeze in plastic bags. To reheat, arrange in a single layer (while still frozen) on a baking sheet and heat in a 350° oven for 12 minutes.

### Shrimp filling

**1 pound medium-size raw shrimp, shelled, deveined, and finely chopped**
**1 can (4 to 6 oz.) water chestnuts, drained and finely chopped**
**2 green onions (including tops), finely chopped**
**2 tablespoons soy sauce**
**⅛ teaspoon garlic salt**

In a bowl, combine shrimp, water chestnuts, green onions, soy, and garlic salt; mix well.

### Pork filling

**1 pound lean ground pork**
**1 can (4 to 6 oz.) water chestnuts, drained and finely chopped**
**2 green onions (including tops), finely chopped**
**1 tablespoon dry sherry**
**¼ teaspoon garlic salt**
**1 teaspoon cornstarch**
**2 tablespoons soy sauce**

In a wide frying pan over medium-high heat, crumble pork and cook, stirring, until browned (about 5 minutes); spoon off excess drippings. Add water chestnuts, green onions, sherry, and garlic salt. In a bowl, combine cornstarch and soy. Add to pan and cook, stirring, until pan juices are thickened. Cool.

### Chorizo sausage & beef filling

**2 chorizo sausages (about 3 oz. each)**
**½ pound lean ground beef**
**1 green onion (including top), finely chopped**
**½ can (4 oz. size) diced green chiles**
**½ cup shredded jack cheese**

Remove casings from chorizos. In a wide frying pan over medium-high heat, crumble chorizos and beef. Cook, stirring, until meat is browned (about 5 minutes); spoon off excess drippings. Stir in green onion, chiles, and cheese. Cook, stirring, until cheese melts. Cool.

## CHINESE DUMPLINGS WITH PEANUT SAUCE

These pork-filled dumplings offer contrasting chewy and silky textures, as well as hot and spicy flavors. Chinese cooks often serve them during their New Year season. In Western menus, these dumplings make a delicious first course or light entrée for any winter meal.

### Peanut sauce

**3 tablespoons creamy-style peanut butter**
**5 tablespoons salad oil**
**¼ cup soy sauce**
**3 tablespoons sugar**
**2 teaspoons sesame oil**
**1 clove garlic, minced or pressed**
**½ teaspoon ground red pepper (cayenne)**

### Pork filling

**½ pound lean ground pork**
**4 water chestnuts, finely chopped**
**1 large green onion (including top), finely chopped**
**1 clove garlic, minced or pressed**
**1½ teaspoons soy sauce**
**1 teaspoon minced fresh ginger**
**1 teaspoon sesame oil**

**½ package (1-lb. size) won ton skins**
**1 egg, lightly beaten**
**6 cups chicken broth or water**
**2 green onions (including tops), thinly sliced**

To make peanut sauce, mix peanut butter and oil until smooth. Add soy, sugar, sesame oil, garlic, and red pepper; stir until smooth. Cover and chill if made ahead, but let come to room temperature before serving.

To make filling, mix pork, water chestnuts, green onion, garlic, soy, ginger, and sesame oil.

Using 1 teaspoon filling for each won ton and moistening edges with egg to seal, fill and wrap won ton according to directions on page 46. Cook according to directions that follow. Or transfer to baking sheets and freeze until firm, then transfer to plastic bags for longer storage in freezer.

*(Continued on next page)*

To cook dumplings, heat chicken broth or water to boiling. Add about 1 dozen won ton, reduce heat, and simmer, uncovered, turning occasionally, until pork filling is no longer pink inside (about 4 minutes). With a slotted spoon, lift dumplings from broth, place in a pan, and cover to keep warm. Continue cooking dumplings until all are cooked and drained.

Serve dumplings in individual shallow bowls. Pour some of the peanut sauce over each serving and sprinkle with some of the sliced green onions. Makes 3 dozen dumplings, enough for 6 first course servings or 3 or 4 entrée servings.

# WON TON SOUP

Won ton soup invites improvisation. You can use any filling in the wrapper and garnish the soup with almost any meat or vegetable. For the first time, though, you might want to try the pork filling used in the preceding recipe. The only rule you need to remember is: cook the won ton in water first so the final soup won't be cloudy.

**3 dozen uncooked, pork-filled won ton (follow directions in preceding recipe for Chinese dumplings with peanut sauce)**
**6 cups chicken broth**
**2 cups coarsely sliced Chinese cabbage (napa cabbage), bok choy, or spinach**
**3 green onions (including tops), thinly sliced**
**1 cup slivered cooked ham or chicken**
**1 teaspoon soy sauce**
**½ teaspoon sesame oil**

Drop won ton into a large kettle of boiling water, reduce heat, and simmer, uncovered, until pork filling is no longer pink inside (about 4 minutes).

While won ton are cooking, bring chicken broth to a boil. Add cabbage (or bok choy) and green onions and cook for 3 minutes. (If using spinach, cook for 2 minutes.) Remove won ton from water with a slotted spoon and drop into hot broth. Add ham,

soy, and sesame oil and heat through. Makes 6 servings.

# SALAMI TURNOVERS

Because you fold them in triangles rather than in the traditional shape, these savory won ton appetizers hold a very generous amount of filling.

**¾ cup *each* finely chopped salami and shredded jack cheese**
**¼ teaspoon garlic powder**
**½ teaspoon oregano leaves**
**½ package (1-lb. size) won ton skins**
**Salad oil**

In a bowl, combine salami, cheese, garlic powder, and oregano; mix lightly. Place 2 teaspoons cheese mixture in center of each won ton skin. Wet your finger with water and lightly moisten all four edges of each skin. Fold in half diagonally to form a triangle, then pinch edges together to seal. Place filled won ton slightly apart in a baking pan and cover with plastic film while you fill the remaining skins. At this point you can cover and refrigerate for as long as 8 hours before cooking.

Into a deep pan, pour oil to a depth of about 1½ inches and heat to 350° on a deep-frying thermometer. Fry 4 to 6 turnovers at a time for 1 minute or until golden. Remove with a slotted spoon and drain on paper towels. Keep warm in a 200° oven until all are cooked. Makes 3 dozen turnovers.

If made ahead, cool fried turnovers, then freeze in plastic bags. To reheat, arrange in a single layer (while still frozen) on a baking sheet and heat in a 350° oven for 12 minutes.

# CHILE-CHEESE TURNOVERS

Though you start with Chinese won ton skins, this hors d'oeuvre captures the essence of Mexican flavor. Serve hot while the filling is still soft and creamy. Choose a mild or spicy-hot dipping sauce to suite your taste.

**8 ounces jack cheese**
**½ package (1-lb. size) won ton skins**
**1 can (4 oz.) diced green chiles**
**Salad oil**
**1 can (7 oz.) red or green chile salsa**
**Salad oil**

Cut cheese in ½ by ½ by 1-inch strips. Place 1 strip cheese and about ½ teaspoon chiles in center of each won ton skin. Wet your finger with water and lightly moisten all four edges of each skin. Fold in half diagonally to form a triangle, then pinch edges together to seal. Place filled won ton slightly apart in a shallow baking pan and cover with plastic film while you fill remaining skins. At this point you can refrigerate for as long as 8 hours before cooking.

Into a deep pan, pour oil to a depth of about 1½ inches and heat to 350° on a deep-frying thermometer. Fry 4 to 6 won ton at a time for 1 minute or until golden. Remove with a slotted spoon and drain on paper towels. Keep warm in a 200° oven until all are cooked. Serve with a dipping sauce of salsa. Makes 3 dozen turnovers.

If made ahead, cool fried turnovers, then freeze in plastic bags. To reheat, arrange in a single layer (while still frozen) on a baking sheet and heat in a 350° oven for 12 minutes.

# EGG ROLLS

Cousin to the won ton skin is the egg roll wrapper that Chinese cooks also fill with a savory mixture and deep fry. The wrappers are available in 1-pound packages in Chinese markets and in supermarkets. For homemade wrappers, the recipe for eggless pasta (page 15), rolled 1/16 inch thick, works best. No homemade pasta will crisp and brown as evenly in deep fat as the packaged wrappers, though, so buy them if you can.

Because of the large size of the wrappers—7 inches square—it takes only a little time to fill egg rolls. If you plan to serve them as snacks, leave them whole, but for appetizers you may wish to cut them in sections before serving.

**Crab or ham filling (directions follow)**
**Sweet and sour sauce (directions follow)**
**1 package (1 lb.) egg roll wrappers**
**1 egg, lightly beaten**
**Salad oil**

Prepare and cool crab or ham filling and sweet and sour sauce. Following the illustrations below, fill and wrap

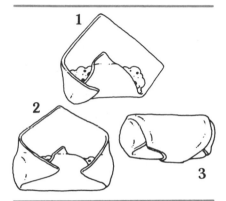

egg rolls. 1. Mound about 2 rounded tablespoons cooled filling across each egg roll wrapper in a 3-inch strip, about 2 inches above the lower corner. Fold bottom corner over filling to cover, then roll over once to enclose filling. 2. Fold over left and right corners, then brush sides and top of triangle with beaten egg. 3. Roll, sealing corner. Place filled egg rolls on a cooky sheet and cover while you fill the remaining wrappers. If made ahead, cover and refrigerate for as long as 8 hours.

In a deep pan, pour salad oil to a depth of 1½ inches and heat to 360° on a deep-frying thermometer. Fry 3 or 4 egg rolls at a time, turning as needed, until golden brown (2 to 3 minutes). Remove with a slotted spoon and drain on paper towels. Keep warm in a 200° oven until all are cooked. Serve with sweet and sour sauce.

If made ahead, cool, cover, and refrigerate (freeze in plastic bags for longer storage). To reheat, place rolls (do not thaw if frozen) in a single layer in a rimmed pan; bake, uncovered, for 15 minutes (25 min-

utes, if frozen) or until hot. Makes about 2 dozen.

## Crab filling

**¾ pound cooked fresh or canned crab**
**1½ teaspoons *each* dry sherry and soy sauce**
**½ teaspoon *each* sugar and salt**
**1 teaspoon *each* cornstarch and sesame oil**
**2 tablespoons salad oil**
**½ teaspoon minced fresh ginger**
**¾ pound bean sprouts**
**¾ cup coarsely chopped mushrooms**
**1 cup thinly sliced celery**
**¾ cup finely chopped bamboo shoots**
**2 green onions (including tops), thinly sliced**

Flake crab, then squeeze to eliminate excess liquid; set aside. In a bowl, combine sherry, soy, sugar, salt, cornstarch, and sesame oil.

Heat a wide frying pan over high heat. When pan is hot, add oil. When oil begins to heat, add ginger. Stir once, then add bean sprouts, mushrooms, celery, and bamboo shoots. Cook, stirring, for 2 minutes. Stir in crab and green onion and cook for 2 minutes. Stir sherry-soy mixture, add to pan, and cook, stirring, until pan juices thicken. Cool.

## Ham filling

**1 tablespoon *each* cornstarch and dry sherry**
**2 teaspoons soy sauce**
**½ teaspoon salt**
**2 tablespoons salad oil**
**1 clove garlic, minced or pressed**
**½ teaspoon grated fresh ginger**
**1 large onion, chopped**
**1 cup thinly sliced celery**
**1 pound cooked ham, cut in matchstick pieces**
**½ cup sliced bamboo shoots, cut in matchstick pieces**
**2 cups finely shredded cabbage**

In a bowl, combine cornstarch, sherry, soy, and salt; set aside. Heat a wide frying pan over high heat. When pan is hot, add oil. When oil begins to heat, add garlic and ginger. Stir once, then add onion and celery; cook, stirring, for 1 minute. Add ham, bamboo shoots, and cabbage;

cook, stirring, for 2 minutes. Stir cornstarch mixture once, add to pan, and cook, stirring, until sauce boils and thickens. Cool.

## Sweet & sour sauce

**3 tablespoons *each* sugar and wine vinegar**
**1 tablespoon *each* cornstarch, soy sauce, and tomato-based chili sauce**
**Dash of ground red pepper (cayenne)**
**½ cup chicken broth**

In a small pan, combine sugar, wine vinegar, cornstarch, soy, chili sauce, red pepper, and chicken broth. Cook, stirring, over high heat until sauce boils and thickens. Cool.

## POT STICKERS

*(Pictured on page 51)*

The Chinese call them *guotie,* but the popular American name for them is "pot stickers." By either name, the savory, filled dumplings make a tasty and substantial first course, lunch, or dinner.

You can make the dough for pot stickers in a food processor or by hand, then choose from the two fillings. Pot stickers freeze well, so you can make them in advance.

**Shrimp or pork-onion filling (directions follow)**
**3 cups all-purpose flour**
**¼ teaspoon salt**
**1 cup boiling water**
**About ¼ cup salad oil**
**About 1⅓ cups chicken broth**
**Soy sauce, vinegar, and chili oil for dipping**

Prepare filling of your choice.

In a bowl, combine flour and salt; mix in water until dough is evenly moistened and begins to hold together. Or mix flour and salt in the food processor and, with motor running, pour water down the feed tube and process until mixture forms a ball. On a lightly floured board, knead dough until very smooth and satiny (about 5 minutes; 1 minute if mixed in processor). Cover and let rest at room temperature for 30 minutes.

To roll out dough by hand, divide dough into 2 equal portions. Keeping one portion covered, roll out other portion until it's about 14 inches in diameter and ⅛ inch thick. Cut out 3½ to 4-inch circles with a round cooky cutter or a clean can with ends removed. Repeat with other portion.

To roll out dough with a pasta machine, roll out one-fourth of the dough at a time and stop at the fourth from the last setting. (This dough is even thicker than the pasta strips used for lasagne.) Cut out 3½ to 4-inch circles with a round cooky cutter or a clean can with ends removed. Repeat with remaining dough.

Dot each circle with about 2 teaspoons of the desired filling. To shape each pot sticker, follow the illustrations below. 1. Fold dough in

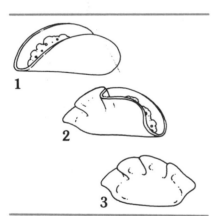

half over filling to form a half moon. 2. Pinch closed about ½ inch of the curved edges. As you continue to seal edges, form 3 tucks along the dough facing you. Continue pressing edges together until entire curve is sealed. 3. Set pot sticker down firmly, seam side up, so that dumpling will sit flat. Cover while you shape remaining pot stickers.

Cook pot stickers according to directions that follow. Or place in a single layer on cooky sheets and freeze until firm, then transfer to plastic bags for longer storage in freezer. Reheat without thawing, as directed below.

Cook pot stickers in batches—a dozen at a time. For each batch, heat 1 tablespoon oil in a heavy, wide frying pan over medium heat. Set pot stickers, seam side up, in pan. Cook until bottoms are golden brown (8 to 10 minutes). Pour in ⅓ cup broth and immediately cover pan tightly. Reduce heat to low and steam pot stickers for 10 minutes (15 minutes if frozen). Uncover and continue cooking until all liquid is absorbed. Using a wide spatula to remove pot stickers from pan, place them, browned side up, on a serving platter. Serve hot with soy, vinegar, and chili oil on the side. Makes about 4 dozen pot stickers, enough for 6 to 10 servings.

## Shrimp filling

**½ pound medium-size raw shrimp, shelled, deveined, and finely chopped**
**½ pound lean ground pork**
**1 cup finely shredded cabbage**
**¼ cup *each* minced green onion and chopped mushrooms**
**1 clove garlic, minced or pressed**
**½ teaspoon salt**
**2 tablespoons oyster sauce or soy sauce**

Combine shrimp, pork, cabbage, onion, mushrooms, garlic, salt, and oyster sauce; mix well.

## Pork-onion filling

**1¼ pounds boneless lean pork, minced**
**2 tablespoons soy sauce**
**1 tablespoon honey**
**2 cloves garlic, minced or pressed**
**⅓ cup minced green onion**
**1 tablespoon salad oil**
**2 teaspoons cornstarch**
**2 tablespoons dry sherry**
**Salt and pepper**

Stir together pork, soy, honey, garlic, and onion. Heat oil in a wide frying pan over high heat. Add pork mixture and cook, stirring, until well browned (6 to 8 minutes). Blend cornstarch and sherry, then stir into pork. Cook, stirring, until mixture boils and thickens. Season with salt and pepper to taste. Cool.

## LUMPIA APPETIZERS

Chinese dishes often have a counterpart in other cuisines. Fried lumpia from the Philippines is one example. This crisp appetizer looks like a miniature egg roll.

**¾ pound lean ground pork**
**1 medium-size onion, chopped**
**3 cloves garlic, minced or pressed**
**⅓ pound medium-size raw shrimp, shelled, deveined, and chopped**
**¾ cup coarsely chopped bean sprouts**
**1½ tablespoons soy sauce**

**1 package (1 lb.) won ton skins**
**1 egg, lightly beaten**
**Salad oil**
**Soy sauce for dipping**

To prepare filling, crumble pork into a wide frying pan. Add onion and garlic and cook, stirring, over medium-high heat until meat is browned and crumbly (about 6 minutes). Add shrimp and cook for 2 minutes. Add bean sprouts and cook for 2 minutes more. Stir in the 1½ tablespoons soy; then cool. Spoon off excess pan juices.

To fill and wrap lumpia, follow directions for folding and wrapping egg rolls on page 49. Use 1 teaspoon filling for each lumpia and moisten edges with egg to seal. If made ahead, cover and refrigerate for as long as 8 hours.

Into a wide frying pan, pour oil to a depth of ¼ inch and place over medium heat. Without crowding, and turning to brown evenly, fry lumpia, for 1 to 2 minutes. Remove with a slotted spoon and drain on paper towels. Keep warm in a 200° oven until all lumpia are cooked. Serve with soy on the side. Makes 6 dozen lumpia.

---

***These Chinese appetizers*** *are called pot stickers because they look as though they'll stick to the pan—actually, you can scoop them up easily. The recipe on page 49 gives you a choice of shrimp or pork filling.*

# Tubes & Giant Shells

## CANNELLONI, MANICOTTI & STUFFED CONCHIGLIE

Cannelloni, manicotti, and conchiglie grande (giant shells) are the featured pastas in this chapter. These three large pastas are grouped because they all can be stuffed with a variety of fillings, then baked. Usually a rich sauce tops them so they won't dry out as they bake. You can serve any of the recipes in this chapter as first courses, or you can increase the number of filled pasta per serving and enjoy them as main dishes.

You've probably ordered cannelloni in a restaurant and been presented with an individual gratin dish containing one or two tubular shapes, reminiscent of enchiladas, wallowing in melted cheese. Once you've poked around in the cheese and taken a bite of the cannelloni, you may have wondered why they tasted so much like crêpes. The reason is simple—they were crêpes.

Replacing pasta with crêpes in this dish is no longer a restaurant shortcut but an accepted procedure. Some might claim that the crêpe version is the original form of Italian cannelloni because crêpes are, after all, a French imitation of the old Italian crespelli. We won't debate the point. One of the cannelloni recipes in this chapter calls specifically for crêpes. The recipe's name is cannelloni country-style—you can pick the country.

The chapter starts with in-structions for making your own pasta squares for cannelloni with the all-purpose pasta recipe on page 8. Whether you make pasta squares or crêpes, we recommend preparing a batch or two and freezing them so you can take out as many as you need for an individual recipe.

Manicotti is usually bought dried. Some versions have ridges, some are smooth. Cooking instructions vary from one manufacturer to another depending on the size and thickness of the pasta. You may even find a version that needs no cooking before stuffing. Giant shells also come in smooth and rigid versions; we've seen some brown whole wheat shells, too.

## MAKING CANNELLONI

Cannelloni are nothing but rectangles of pasta rolled around a filling. Pasta rectangles are very easy to cut. Start by making a pasta dough, such as all-purpose pasta (page 8) or semolina pasta (page 10). Spinach pasta (page 10) and whole wheat pasta (page 8) would work, too. Make a full dough recipe and freeze uncooked cannelloni rectangles to be used as needed. After mixing and kneading, roll the dough out by machine or by hand.

By machine, roll out one-fourth of the dough at a time to the third from the last setting, as you would for lasagne. Try to roll out the dough as wide as the machine will allow. If the dough emerges in a narrow strip, fold it in thirds, reset the rollers to the widest setting, and put the wide, folded side through the rollers. That should make the dough stretch to the full width of the machine and produce a strip about 4 inches wide. Cut each strip into as many 5-inch lengths as possible. Any short pieces at the end can be rolled out with the next portion of dough. Flour after cutting.

If you roll out the dough by hand, work with one-fourth of the dough at a time. Roll out each piece into a rectangle about 10 inches wide and as long as you can roll it. The dough should be about $\frac{1}{16}$ inch thick, as for lasagne. Cut the rectangle in half, lengthwise. Cut each 5-inch-wide strip into as many 4-inch lengths as possible. If you end up with a short piece at the end, roll it out with the next fourth of the dough. Lightly flour the rectangles as you cut them.

Once all the dough has been cut into rectangles, let the cannelloni dry until leathery but not brittle (probably 15 to 30 minutes). Package them by layering pieces of plastic wrap between rectangles. Sprinkle each layer with flour if the pasta is sticky. Place stacks of cannelloni in airtight bags and refrigerate overnight or freeze for as long as 2 months, using as needed.

**What size pan?** A full recipe of cannelloni requires a rather large pan or shallow casserole that is suitable for both baking and serving. It may be easier for you to use several small containers. Choose among the following: one large, shallow container about 12 by 15 inches; two shallow containers, each at least 6 by 15 inches; or 6 to 8 individual containers, each about 3 by 6 inches.

## CANNELLONI ROMA

In traditional cannelloni there are four separately prepared elements: the filling, the fresh noodles in which it is enclosed, the cheese that swaths and protects the filled noodle as it heats, and, finally, the sauce. Each can be prepared at least a day ahead, then assembled just before serving.

### Filling

**4 tablespoons butter or margarine**
**1 small clove garlic, peeled**
**1 large onion, coarsely chopped**
**1¼ pounds chicken thighs, skinned, boned, and cut in 2-inch pieces**
**½ pound boneless veal, cut in 2-inch pieces**
**1 cup ricotta cheese**
**½ cup grated Parmesan cheese**
**1 egg**
**¾ teaspoon salt**
**⅛ teaspoon ground nutmeg**

### White sauce

**4 tablespoons butter or margarine**
**1½ tablespoons all-purpose flour**
**1½ cups chicken broth**
**1 cup milk**

### Tomato sauce

**1½ tablespoons butter or margarine**
**2 tablespoons chopped shallots or white part of green onions**
**1 can (about 1 lb.) Italian-style tomatoes**
**½ cup chicken broth**
**½ teaspoon *each* dry basil and salt**

**16 unfilled cannelloni (page 52)**
**Boiling salted water**
**1½ pounds teleme or jack cheese**

To make filling, melt butter in a wide frying pan over medium heat. Add garlic and onion and cook until onion is limp. Add chicken and veal and stir to coat each piece with butter. Cover pan, reduce heat to medium-low, and cook until meat is tender (about 35 minutes).

Using a food processor or the finest blade of a meat grinder, finely chop meat mixture. Blend with ricotta, Parmesan, egg, salt, and nutmeg. (If made ahead, blend meat mixture with ricotta, Parmesan, salt, and nutmeg. Cover and refrigerate. Mix in egg just before filling.)

To make white sauce, melt butter in a 2-quart pan over medium heat. Stir in flour and cook, stirring, until bubbly. Remove pan from heat and stir in chicken broth and milk. Return to heat and cook, stirring, until sauce is smooth and thickened.

To make tomato sauce, melt butter in a 2-quart pan over medium-high heat. Add shallots and cook until soft. Cut tomatoes in half and squeeze out seeds (strain juice); finely chop tomatoes. Add tomatoes and juice to pan along with chicken broth, basil, and salt. Stirring occasionally, simmer, uncovered, until sauce is thick (about 30 minutes).

Cook fresh or frozen pasta, 4 or 5 rectangles at a time, in a large kettle of boiling salted water until al dente (2 to 3 minutes). Remove with a slotted spoon, rinse with cold water, and drain. When all pasta is cooked, fill by placing about ¼ cup meat filling in a row along one long edge of each rectangle; roll to enclose.

Stir tomato sauce into white sauce until well blended. Spread half the sauce mixture in a buttered baking pan (see "What size pan," page 52). Place filled cannelloni, seam side down and slightly apart, in sauce. Pour remaining sauce mixture over cannelloni. Top each cannelloni with a slice of teleme just slightly longer and wider than the top of each noodle. If made ahead, cover and refrigerate until next day.

Bake, uncovered, in a 400° oven until hot and bubbly and cheese melts (about 30 minutes). Makes 8 servings of 2 cannelloni each.

## SEAFOOD CANNELLONI

This isn't a simple dish to prepare, but every bite makes your efforts worthwhile, and there are short cuts you can take to help matters along. For instance, a batch of cannelloni rectangles can be made ahead, so all you have to do is take 16 of them from the freezer and plop them into boiling salted water. In fact, the entire dish can be made a day in advance, so you can relax and enjoy it with your guests.

There's so much to enjoy in this dish. Vegetable-enriched tomato sauce goes on the bottom, then the crab and shrimp-filled tubes of cannelloni, followed by a combination of fontina cheese and white sauce with inspired touches of nutmeg, white pepper, and vermouth.

### Tomato sauce

**2 tablespoons butter or margarine**
**1 medium-size onion, finely chopped**
**1 medium-size carrot, shredded**
**¼ cup chopped parsley**
**1 can (about 1 lb.) tomatoes**
**1 cup chicken broth**
**1 teaspoon dry basil**

### White sauce

**¼ cup butter or margarine**
**1 small onion, finely chopped**
**2 tablespoons all-purpose flour**
**⅛ teaspoon *each* ground nutmeg and white pepper**
**¾ cup *each* milk and chicken broth**
**1 cup (4 oz.) shredded fontina cheese**
**2 tablespoons dry vermouth**

### Filling

**¾ pound cooked or canned crab, flaked**
**½ pound small cooked shrimp**
**3 green onions (including tops), thinly sliced**
**1 cup (4 oz.) shredded fontina cheese**

**16 unfilled cannelloni (page 52)**
**Boiling salted water**
**½ cup grated Parmesan cheese**

*(Continued on page 55)*

*. . . Seafood Cannelloni (cont'd.)*

To make tomato sauce, melt butter in a wide frying pan over medium-high heat. Add onion and carrot and cook until onion is limp and lightly browned. Add parsley, tomatoes and their liquid (break up tomatoes with a spoon), chicken broth, and basil. Bring to a boil, reduce heat, cover, and simmer for 15 minutes. Uncover and continue cooking, stirring occasionally, until sauce is thickened (about 30 minutes).

To make white sauce, melt butter in a 2-quart pan over medium heat. Add onion and cook until limp. Blend in flour, nutmeg, and pepper. Remove pan from heat and gradually stir in milk and chicken broth. Return to heat and cook, stirring constantly, until sauce is smooth and thickened. Stir in fontina until melted. Mix in vermouth.

To make filling, combine crab, shrimp, green onions, and fontina; mix lightly.

Cook fresh or frozen pasta, 4 or 5 rectangles at a time, in a large kettle of boiling salted water until al dente (2 to 3 minutes). Remove with a slotted spoon, rinse with cold water, and drain. When all pasta is cooked, fill by placing about ¼ cup crab filling in a row along one long edge of each rectangle; roll to enclose filling.

Spread tomato sauce in a buttered baking pan (see "What size pan," page 52). Place filled cannelloni, seam side down and slightly apart, in sauce. Pour white sauce evenly over cannelloni. Sprinkle with Parmesan.

Bake, uncovered, in a 400° oven until hot and bubbly and cheese is lightly browned (30 to 35 minutes). Makes 8 servings of 2 cannelloni each.

*Ricotta-stuffed giant shells (recipe on page 56) follow an antipasto course of Italian salami, pickled vegetables, and bread sticks for a light supper with an Italian flair.*

# CANNELLONI COUNTRY-STYLE

Crêpes replace pasta in this quick version of cannelloni. It's even quicker if you've made and frozen crêpes in advance. Then you just have to thaw as many as you need. The garlic-fragrant cheese inside this crêpe-cannelloni is smooth and creamy, while the sauce is textured with ground beef, carrot, and onion—rather the reverse of the usual cannelloni with meat on the inside and creamy sauce on the outside.

Two cannelloni make a moderate main-course serving. A spinach salad, a serve-yourself cheese board accompanied by crusty French bread, plenty of robust red wine, then sherbet topped with fresh fruit for dessert could complete your supper.

## Meat sauce

**1 tablespoon salad oil**
**1 pound lean ground beef**
**1 medium-size onion, finely chopped**
**1 cup chopped parsley**
**1 medium-size carrot, finely chopped**
**1 can (6 oz.) tomato paste**
**1 can (about 1 lb.) Italian-style tomatoes**
**1 can (14 oz.) chicken broth**
**1 teaspoon dry basil**
**½ teaspoon salt**
**¼ teaspoon pepper**

## Crêpes

**1 cup milk**
**3 eggs**
**⅔ cup all-purpose flour**
**About 4 teaspoons butter or margarine**

## Filling

**2 tablespoons butter or margarine**
**1 tablespoon minced or pressed garlic**
**2 cups chopped parsley**
**1 pound jack or teleme cheese**

## Topping

**1 to 1½ cups (3 to 4½ oz.) grated Parmesan cheese**

To make sauce, pour oil into a Dutch oven or deep frying pan over medium-high heat. Crumble in meat and cook, stirring, until it loses all pink color. Add onion, parsley, and carrot and cook until carrot is soft.

Stir in tomato paste. Add tomatoes and their liquid (break up tomatoes with a spoon), chicken broth, basil, salt, and pepper. Boil rapidly, stirring to prevent sticking, until thickened (about 10 minutes). If made ahead, cool, cover, and refrigerate.

To make crêpes, whirl milk, eggs, and flour in a blender until smooth. (Or blend eggs and milk with a wire whip; add flour and mix until smooth.) Let rest at room temperature for at least 1 hour.

Place a 6 or 7-inch crêpe pan (or other flat-bottom frying pan) on medium heat. When hot, add ¼ teaspoon butter and swirl to coat surface. Stir batter and pour in about 2 tablespoons, quickly tilting pan so batter flows over entire flat surface. Cook until surface of batter is dry and edge is lightly browned. Turn and brown other side. Turn out onto a plate, stacking crêpes.

If you don't plan to use them within a few hours, place wax paper between crêpes, package airtight, and refrigerate for as long as 1 week or freeze for longer storage. Allow crêpes to come to room temperature before separating them; they tear if cold.

To make filling, melt butter in a wide frying pan over low heat. Add garlic and cook, stirring, until garlic is golden (do not brown). Add parsley and cook for 1 minute. Cut jack cheese in 16 equal sticks. Divide parsley mixture equally among crêpes. Lay a cheese stick on each crêpe, then roll to enclose.

Spread half the meat sauce in a baking pan (see "What size pan," page 52). Place filled crêpes, seam side down and slightly apart, in meat sauce. Spoon remaining sauce over crêpes to cover, then sprinkle evenly with Parmesan. If made ahead, cover and refrigerate until next day.

Bake, uncovered, in a 450° oven for 12 to 15 minutes or until sauce is bubbling. Makes 8 servings of 2 cannelloni each.

# HAM MANICOTTI WITH CHEESE SAUCE

You make a kind of deviled ham filling for this manicotti, combining finely chopped ham, cottage cheese, and half a spice cabinet of seasonings—marjoram, sage, garlic salt, hot pepper, and a little Worcestershire. A creamy cheese sauce surrounds the manicotti.

## Filling

**1 egg**
**1 cup small curd cottage cheese**
**2 cups ground cooked ham**
**2 green onions (including tops), finely chopped**
**½ teaspoon *each* Worcestershire, rubbed sage, and marjoram**
**¼ teaspoon garlic salt**
**3 drops liquid hot pepper seasoning**

## Cheese sauce

**3 tablespoons butter or margarine**
**3 tablespoons all-purpose flour**
**1 cup milk**
**½ cup chicken broth**
**1 tablespoon tomato paste**
**Dash *each* of ground nutmeg and ground red pepper (cayenne)**
**2 tablespoons *each* shredded Swiss cheese and grated Parmesan cheese**

**8 unfilled manicotti**
**Boiling salted water**
**½ cup shredded Swiss cheese**

To make filling, beat egg into cottage cheese. Stir in ham, onion, Worcestershire, sage, marjoram, garlic salt, and hot pepper seasoning; mix well.

To make sauce, melt butter in a 1-quart pan over medium heat. Add flour and stir until bubbly. Remove pan from heat and stir in milk and chicken broth. Return to heat and cook, stirring, until sauce is smooth and thickened. Stir in tomato paste, nutmeg, red pepper, Swiss cheese, and Parmesan. Cook until cheese melts.

Following package directions, cook manicotti in a large kettle of boiling salted water until al dente. Drain, rinse with cold water, and drain again. Stuff with ham filling.

Spread one-fourth of sauce in a 9 by 13-inch baking dish. Arrange filled manicotti, side by side, in sauce. Spoon on remaining sauce and sprinkle with the ½ cup Swiss cheese. If made ahead, cover and refrigerate until next day. Bake, covered, in a 350° oven until hot and bubbly (about 30 minutes). Makes 4 servings of 2 manicotti each.

# SALMON MANICOTTI

Divinely creamy teleme melting over salmon-stuffed manicotti and spilling into the wine-flavored tomato sauce . . . it's a luscious dish that tastes much more complicated than it is. Enjoy it as a starter or main dish.

## Tomato sauce

**3 tablespoons butter or margarine**
**1 large onion, chopped**
**1 large green pepper, seeded and chopped**
**1 large can (1 lb. 12 oz.) tomatoes**
**1 cup dry white wine**
**½ teaspoon salt**
**Dash of pepper**

## Filling

**2 cups (1 lb.) ricotta cheese**
**2 egg yolks**
**2 tablespoons chopped parsley**
**½ teaspoon *each* salt, thyme leaves, and dry basil**
**Dash of pepper**
**2 cups flaked cooked salmon or 1 can (1 lb.) salmon**

**8 unfilled manicotti**
**Boiling salted water**
**½ pound teleme or jack cheese, cut into 8 slices**
**¼ cup grated Parmesan cheese**

To make sauce, melt butter in a 2-quart pan over medium-high heat. Add onion and green pepper and cook until onion is limp. Add tomatoes and their liquid (break up tomatoes with a spoon), wine, salt, and pepper. Reduce heat and simmer, uncovered, stirring occasionally, until sauce is thickened (about 20 minutes).

To make filling, combine ricotta, egg yolks, parsley, salt, thyme, basil, and pepper. Fold in salmon (if you use canned salmon, drain and remove skin and bones first).

Following package directions, cook manicotti in a large kettle of boiling salted water until al dente. Drain, rinse with cold water, and drain again. Stuff with salmon filling. Spread one-fourth of sauce in 9 by 13-inch baking dish. Arrange filled manicotti side by side in sauce, then cover with remaining sauce. Top each filled manicotti with a slice of teleme. If made ahead, cover and refrigerate until next day.

Bake, covered, in a 350° oven until hot and bubbly (about 30 minutes). Sprinkle with Parmesan. Makes 4 servings of 2 manicotti each.

# RICOTTA-STUFFED GIANT SHELLS

*(Pictured on page 54)*

That ubiquitous Italian couple—ricotta and spinach—turns up in shells this time. Flavored with onion, garlic, parsley, and oregano, the filling goes into two dozen giant shells for a tasty first course or main dish. Topped with a tomato and mushroom sauce, the whole dish is delightful.

**4 cups Italian mushroom gravy (page 69)**
**1 package (10 or 12 oz.) frozen chopped spinach, thawed**
**3 tablespoons butter or margarine**
**1 small onion, finely chopped**
**1 clove garlic, minced or pressed**
**2 eggs**
**2 cups (1 lb.) ricotta cheese**
**¼ cup grated Parmesan cheese**
**1 tablespoon chopped parsley**
**½ teaspoon *each* oregano leaves and salt**
**Dash of pepper**
**24 giant shells**
**Boiling salted water**
**Grated Parmesan cheese**

Make Italian mushroom gravy and refrigerate until needed.

With your hands, press out as much water as possible from spinach.

In a wide frying pan over medium heat, melt butter. Add onion and garlic and cook until onion is limp. Add spinach and cook for 3 minutes. Cool. Stir eggs into ricotta until well blended, then stir in spinach mixture, Parmesan, parsley, oregano, salt, and pepper.

Following package directions, cook giant shells in a large kettle of boiling salted water until al dente. Drain, rinse with cold water, and drain again. Stuff each shell with 3 tablespoons of the spinach-cheese mixture.

Pour half the Italian mushroom gravy into an 8 by 12-inch baking dish. Arrange filled shells side by side in sauce. Spoon remaining sauce over top. If made ahead, cover and refrigerate until next day. Bake, covered, in a 350° oven until hot and bubbly (about 30 minutes). Pass Parmesan at the table. Makes 4 or 5 main-dish servings.

## CREAMY CLAM SHELLS

Chopped clams, sliced mushrooms, and onions cuddle in whipping cream, white wine, and egg yolks to make a rich filling for giant shells. Instead of being coated with a sauce —which they hardly need—these shells are drizzled with butter and sprinkled with crumbs before baking.

**2 cans (6½ oz. *each*) chopped clams**
**¼ cup *each* dry white wine and whipping cream**
**6 tablespoons butter or margarine**
**½ cup chopped green onions (including tops)**
**½ pound mushrooms, sliced**
**1 tablespoon all-purpose flour**
**6 tablespoons grated Parmesan cheese**
**3 egg yolks, beaten**
**1 teaspoon lemon juice**
**18 giant shells**
   **Boiling salted water**
   **About 2 tablespoons melted butter or margarine**
**⅓ cup fine dry bread crumbs**

Drain clams well, reserving clam juice. Combine ½ cup of clam juice with wine and cream. Set aside remaining clam juice.

In a wide frying pan over medium-high heat, melt 4 tablespoons of the butter. Add onion and mushrooms and cook until onion is limp and all liquid from mushrooms has evaporated. Stir in flour and cook, stirring, until bubbly. Pour in clam juice mixture and cook, stirring, until sauce is smooth and thickened. Add drained clams and 3 tablespoons of the Parmesan. Bring mixture to a boil, stirring; then remove from heat. Beat some of the hot mixture into egg yolks, then stir egg mixture into hot mixture in pan. Reduce heat to medium and cook, stirring constantly, until thickened (do not boil). Stir in lemon juice.

Following package directions, cook giant shells in a large kettle of boiling salted water until al dente. Drain, rinse with cold water, and drain again. Brush outside of each shell with melted butter, then fill each shell with about 2 tablespoons filling. Place filled shells side by side in a buttered 8 by 12-inch baking dish. Melt remaining 2 tablespoons butter; mix with bread crumbs and remaining 3 tablespoons Parmesan until well blended. Sprinkle crumb mixture evenly over shells. Pour reserved clam juice into dish around shells. If made ahead, cover and refrigerate until next day.

Bake, covered, in a 350° oven until hot and bubbly (about 30 minutes). Makes 4 main-dish servings.

## CHEESE & SAUSAGE-STUFFED SHELLS

Here's a dish you can turn out rather quickly to prove once again what a super chef you are. The stuffing for the shells couldn't be simpler—just crumbled browned sausages, egg, and ricotta, seasoned with Parmesan and parsley. The shells are complemented by a Swiss chard sauce. You could use the same filling and sauce for manicotti, too.

**2 mild Italian sausages (3 oz. *each*)**
**1 egg**
**1 cup ricotta cheese**
**2 tablespoons grated Parmesan cheese**
**¼ teaspoon salt**
**1 tablespoon chopped parsley**
**12 whole wheat, spinach, or regular giant shells, or 8 unfilled manicotti**
   **Boiling salted water**
**2 cups Swiss chard sauce (page 69)**
**¼ cup grated Parmesan cheese**

Remove casings from sausages. Crumble meat into a wide frying pan and cook over medium heat until brown; pour off pan drippings.

Beat egg into ricotta, then combine with sausage, Parmesan, salt, and parsley.

Following package directions, cook giant shells or manicotti in a large kettle of boiling salted water until al dente. Drain, rinse with cold water, and drain again. Stuff with sausage-cheese mixture.

Spread half the Swiss chard sauce in an 8-inch-square baking dish. Arrange pasta side by side in sauce. Spoon remaining sauce over top.

Bake, covered, in a 350° oven until hot and bubbly (about 30 minutes). Sprinkle with Parmesan before serving. Makes 3 or 4 servings.

# Strands

## SPAGHETTI, VERMICELLI, SOBA & UDON

Spaghetti—or as the kids say, busketti—is the featured pasta strand in this chapter. You'll find spaghetti sauced with squid, mussels, and marinara sauce, not to mention baked with crab and turkey.

Fusilli (twisty strands), linguine (oval strands), and vermicelli (very fine strands) are the other Italian pastas that appear in this section. Oriental strands, like udon and soba, as well as Oriental-style recipes using vermicelli, conclude the chapter. Most of the recipes call for dried, packaged pasta because cylindrical strands are virtually impossible to make at home.

By the time you've sampled both Western and Oriental recipes, the controversy over who invented spaghetti—Italy or China—will matter not at all.

The Oriental way with pasta strands is so different from the Western way that it seems silly to try to claim that one tradition was derived from the other. It's more fun to appreciate each tradition's special qualities than to argue over who did it first. Besides, the story that Marco Polo discovered spaghetti in China sounds too slick to be true, especially the version in which a sailor named Spaghetti makes the great discovery.

Though Western and Oriental methods of eating pasta strands are as different as forks and chopsticks, they look equally humorous. The accepted Italian way to eat spaghetti is to twirl a modest amount on your fork, using the plate (not a large spoon) as the twirling base. Any loose strands are inhaled with gusto.

The Oriental method for eating spaghetti-type strands is even more like vacuuming than the Western method. Fortunately, you don't have to twirl the strands on the chopsticks. Instead, you use the chopsticks to hold up the strands as you vacuum them into your mouth in a steady stream.

## OLD-FASHIONED MEATBALLS & SPAGHETTI

*(Pictured on facing page)*

Cooks from Southern Italy take pride in their meatballs. They make them plump and light—large enough to be important—then drench them in a robust, herby tomato gravy. What better way to cloak a steaming mound of spaghetti.

This recipe makes a large quantity of meatballs and gravy, so if you don't serve it all at one time, freeze the remainder. Then you can repeat this recipe or perhaps use the meatballs for sandwiches and the sauce on another pasta or as the base for a meat sauce—the possibilities are endless.

Neapolitan gravy (directions follow)
5 slices day-old sweet French bread, crusts removed
2 pounds ground chuck
1 cup (3 oz.) grated Parmesan cheese
1 large onion, finely chopped
½ cup chopped parsley
1 teaspoon salt
½ teaspoon pepper
1 teaspoon oregano leaves
2 teaspoons dry basil
3 cloves garlic, minced or pressed
3 eggs
3 tablespoons olive oil or salad oil
2 to 3 ounces spaghetti per person
Boiling salted water
Grated Parmesan cheese

Combine ingredients for Neapolitan gravy; set aside.

In a food processor or blender, whirl bread to make crumbs (you should have 2 cups lightly packed crumbs). In a large bowl, mix together crumbs, chuck, cheese, onion, parsley, salt, pepper, oregano, basil, garlic, and eggs; blend well. Form mixture into 1½-inch meatballs.

*(Continued on page 60)*

***King of spaghetti mountain!***
*Behemoth meatballs in a robust tomato sauce will make the kids smile and everyone proclaim old-fashioned meatballs and spaghetti the best. The recipe is on this page.*

Heat olive oil in a wide frying pan over medium heat. Add meatballs and brown on all sides, shaking pan frequently so balls keep their round shape. Drain briefly on paper towels. Add meatballs to gravy. Bring to a boil, then reduce heat, cover, and simmer for 45 minutes.

Following package directions, cook spaghetti in a large kettle of boiling salted water until al dente; then drain. Transfer spaghetti to a deep serving dish and pour sauce with meatballs over spaghetti. Pass grated cheese at the table. Makes about 4 dozen meatballs and 2½ quarts gravy.

**Neapolitan gravy.** In a large kettle or Dutch oven, combine 2 cans (1 lb. 12 oz. *each*) **tomato purée**, 2 cloves **garlic** (minced or pressed), ½ cup chopped **parsley**, ½ pound **mushrooms** (sliced), ¾ cup **dry red wine**, 2 tablespoons **dry basil**, 1 tablespoon **oregano leaves**, 2 teaspoons **salt**, 1 teaspoon **sugar**, ½ teaspoon **pepper**, and 1½ cups **water**.

## MARINARA SPAGHETTI

You don't have to brown the pork cubes for this recipe; they simmer to fork-tender succulence in an herb-seasoned tomato sauce. Select a dry red wine to add to the sauce, then enjoy the rest of the bottle with this main-dish spaghetti.

2 tablespoons olive oil
1 medium-size onion, finely chopped
1 large carrot, finely chopped
1 large green pepper, seeded and finely chopped
4 cloves garlic, minced or pressed
1 can (1 lb.) tomato purée
3 cans (8 oz. *each*) tomato sauce
½ cup dry red wine
2 teaspoons salt
1 tablespoon sugar
¼ teaspoon pepper
⅛ teaspoon ground red pepper (cayenne)
1 teaspoon *each* dry rosemary, oregano leaves, and dry basil
1 bay leaf
2 pounds lean boneless pork shoulder, cut in ½-inch cubes
¼ pound mushrooms, sliced
1 pound spaghetti or vermicelli
Boiling salted water
Grated Parmesan or Romano cheese

Heat olive oil in a 6 to 8-quart kettle over medium heat. Add onion, carrot, green pepper, and garlic; cook until vegetables are tender. Add tomato purée, tomato sauce, red wine, salt, sugar, pepper, red pepper, rosemary, oregano, basil, bay leaf, and pork. Bring to a boil, reduce heat, cover, and simmer for 1½ hours or until pork is fork-tender. Add mushrooms and simmer, uncovered, for about 10 minutes more. Remove bay leaf.

Following package directions, cook spaghetti in a large kettle of boiling salted water until al dente; drain and toss with grated cheese to taste. Arrange spaghetti on a serving dish, ladle some sauce over it, and serve. (Freeze any remaining sauce.) Makes 6 to 8 servings.

## GREEK MEATBALLS & SPAGHETTI

Since so much ancient Roman culture was borrowed from the Greeks, it's only fair that Greek cookery borrow something back from the Italians. In this case, meatballs and spaghetti turn into a Greek dish when the meatballs are two-thirds beef and one-third lamb, and are spiced with the delicate flavor of mint. The meatballs simmer in a light tomato sauce, and a garlicky parsley-flavored yogurt sauce is passed separately at the table to spoon over individual servings.

Yogurt sauce (directions follow)
1 pound lean ground beef
½ pound lean ground lamb
1½ tablespoons finely chopped fresh mint or 2 teaspoons dry mint
½ cup fresh bread crumbs
2 eggs
1 medium-size onion, finely chopped
1¼ teaspoons salt
⅛ teaspoon pepper
All-purpose flour
2 tablespoons salad oil
1 can (about 1 lb.) tomatoes
½ teaspoon dry basil
12 ounces spaghetti
Boiling salted water

Make yogurt sauce and refrigerate until needed.

In a bowl, combine beef, lamb, mint, bread crumbs, eggs, onion, salt, and pepper; mix well. Shape mixture into walnut-size meatballs. Roll balls in flour and shake off excess.

In a wide frying pan, heat oil over medium-high heat. Brown meatballs, a portion at a time, until they are browned on all sides; pour off and discard pan drippings. Add tomatoes and their liquid (break up tomatoes

with a spoon) and basil. Cover and simmer for 15 minutes or until meatballs are tender.

Following package directions, cook spaghetti in a large kettle of boiling salted water until al dente; then drain. Transfer spaghetti to a deep serving dish and pour sauce and meatballs over spaghetti. Pass a bowl of yogurt sauce to spoon over each serving. Makes 4 to 5 servings.

**Yogurt sauce.** In a small bowl, combine 1 cup **unflavored yogurt,** 1 clove **garlic** (minced or pressed), and ¼ cup chopped **parsley;** mix well.

## CHICKEN CACCIATORE

*(Pictured on page 67)*

*Cacciatore* means "hunters' style," and a dish with this name usually includes tomatoes, onions, green peppers, and sometimes mushrooms. You'll find versions of this famous dish made with red wine, white wine, or dry sherry. Our cacciatore uses a small amount of a dry white wine. Traditionally, this entrée is served on pasta strands. You can complete a supper menu with bread sticks, a salad, wine, and fruit.

> 2 tablespoons olive oil or salad oil
> 4 tablespoons butter or margarine
> 3-pound broiler-fryer chicken, cut in pieces
> ½ pound mushrooms, sliced
> 1 medium-size onion, chopped
> 2 green peppers, seeded and chopped
> 2 cloves garlic, minced or pressed
> 2 tablespoons chopped parsley
> ½ cup water
> ½ cup dry white wine or chicken broth
> 1 can (6 oz.) tomato paste
> 1½ teaspoons salt
> ¼ teaspoon *each* marjoram, oregano, and thyme leaves
> 1 chicken bouillon cube or 1 teaspoon chicken-flavored stock base
> 8 ounces fusilli or spaghetti Boiling salted water

Heat oil and 2 tablespoons of the butter in a wide frying pan over medium-high heat. Add chicken pieces and cook, turning, until browned on all sides; remove from pan and set aside. Pour off and discard all but 3 tablespoons of the pan drippings.

Add mushrooms, onion, green peppers, and garlic to pan; reduce heat to medium and cook, stirring, until onion is limp. Add parsley, water, wine, tomato paste, salt, marjoram, oregano, thyme, and bouillon cube to pan; stir until mixed and cube is dissolved. Return chicken (except breast pieces) to pan. Bring to a boil, reduce heat, cover, and simmer for 25 minutes. Add breast pieces and continue to simmer, covered, for about 20 more minutes or until meat is no longer pink in thickest part (cut a small gash to test).

Just before serving, follow package directions and cook fusilli in a large kettle of boiling salted water until al dente; then drain. Toss fusilli with remaining 2 tablespoons butter. Arrange chicken in center of a deep serving plate, place fusilli around chicken, and spoon sauce over chicken. Makes 4 or 5 servings.

## SPAGHETTI WITH WHITE CLAM SAUCE

Clam sauce and spaghetti is a traditional Italian combination and, like American clam chowder, it comes in red and white versions. With canned clams in your pantry, you can make this white version on a moment's notice for a festive company meal.

> ½ cup butter
> ¼ cup olive oil
> 4 cloves garlic, minced or pressed
> 3 cans (6½ oz. *each*) chopped clams
> 1 teaspoon *each* oregano leaves and dry basil (or 1 tablespoon fresh basil)
> ¼ teaspoon crushed red pepper
> 1½ cups chopped parsley
> 1 pound spaghetti or linguine Boiling salted water

In a 2-quart pan over medium-low heat, melt butter in olive oil. Add garlic and cook until golden; do not let garlic burn. Drain the juice from 2 of the cans of clams into butter mixture; reserve juice from the third can for other uses. Add oregano, basil, red pepper, and parsley to pan; simmer for 5 minutes. Add drained clams and heat through.

Meanwhile, following package directions, cook spaghetti in a large kettle of boiling salted water until al dente; then drain. Toss clam sauce with spaghetti. Makes 5 or 6 main-dish servings.

## SPAGHETTI WITH RED CLAM SAUCE

When fresh clams are in season, you may wish to try this red-sauced version garnished with clams in their shells. Italians enjoy *pasta con vongole* (pasta with clams) made with the tiny clams found in the southern waters of Italy.

> ¼ cup *each* olive oil and butter
> 3 tablespoons finely chopped parsley
> 1 to 2 cloves garlic, minced or pressed
> 3 medium-size tomatoes, peeled, seeded, and chopped
> ¼ teaspoon salt
> ⅛ teaspoon pepper
> Few drops liquid hot pepper seasoning
> ¼ teaspoon oregano leaves
> 3 to 4 dozen small hard-shell clams
> 2 tablespoons water
> 8 ounces spaghetti or linguine Boiling salted water

Heat olive oil and butter in a wide frying pan over medium heat. Add parsley and garlic and cook for 2 minutes. Add tomatoes, salt, pepper, liquid hot pepper seasoning, and oregano. Simmer gently, stirring occasionally, for about 10 minutes; then reduce heat to keep warm.

Meanwhile, scrub clams and rinse well. Put clams and the 2 tablespoons water into a heavy pan. Cover and simmer just until clams open (5 to 10 minutes). When cool

*(Continued on page 63)*

... *Spaghetti with Red Clam Sauce (cont'd.)*

enough to handle, pluck whole clams from shells and put into sauce; save some clams in their shells for garnish, if you wish. Strain clam juices from pan through a muslin cloth and add juices to sauce.

Following package directions, cook spaghetti in a large kettle of boiling salted water until al dente; then drain. Return spaghetti to kettle, pour sauce over spaghetti, and toss. Turn into a serving bowl. Makes 4 main-dish servings.

## PERCIATELLE WITH MUSSELS MARINARA

*(Pictured on facing page)*

Wait until mussels are in season, then make this lightly sauced entrée. Scrubbing the mussels is the hardest part of the preparation—and while you're scrubbing, be sure to discard any mussels that are not firmly closed. The sauce is a simple simmer of tomatoes, oregano, pepper, parsley, and wine. The combination of bouncy perciatelle—a fat strand with a hole in the middle—and mussels calls for a wide napkin tucked under the chin.

1 quart mussels in the shells
3 tablespoons olive oil
½ small onion, chopped
1 clove garlic, minced or pressed
1 can (about 1 lb.) Italian-style tomatoes
½ teaspoon oregano leaves
  Dash of ground red pepper (cayenne)
2 tablespoons chopped parsley
¼ cup dry white wine
8 ounces perciatelle or thick spaghetti
  Boiling salted water

*Perky perciatelle and mussels make a handsome dish when lightly dressed in a quick marinara sauce. Be sure your guests are well protected with wide napkins tucked under their chins— perciatelle (a fat strand pierced in the middle) tends to bounce off the fork, and mussels aren't the tidiest of foods, either. The recipe for perciatelle and mussels marinara is above.*

Scrub mussels with a stiff brush under running water. With a knife, scrape off tuft of hairs, or beard, which protrudes from one side of the closed shell.

Heat oil in a Dutch oven over medium heat. When oil is hot, add onion and garlic and cook until onion is limp. Add tomatoes and their liquid (break up tomatoes with a spoon), oregano, red pepper, parsley, and wine. Reduce heat and simmer, uncovered, for 10 minutes, stirring occasionally. Add mussels and stir to coat with sauce. Cover and simmer just until mussels have opened (5 to 8 minutes). Discard any that don't open.

Following package directions, cook pasta in a large kettle of boiling salted water until al dente; then drain. Return pasta to kettle, pour over mussels and sauce, and lift and mix gently so all pasta is coated with sauce. Turn into a serving bowl. Makes 4 servings.

## SPAGHETTI WITH SQUID

Tender bites of squid flavor this subtle spaghetti sauce. If squid is new to you, think of it as a delicately flavored, economical substitute for abalone.

1 pound squid, fresh or frozen and thawed
1 large onion, chopped
1 large clove garlic, minced or pressed
½ medium-size green pepper, seeded and chopped
3 tablespoons olive oil or salad oil
1 can (about 1 lb.) Italian-style tomatoes
½ teaspoon *each* chervil, dry basil, and salt
¼ teaspoon *each* dry rosemary and pepper
2 tablespoons chopped parsley
8 ounces spaghetti or vermicelli
  Boiling salted water

To clean squid, peel off and discard the thin speckled membrane from the mantle to expose the pure white meat of the mantle. Pull out the long transparent shell from inside the

mantle and discard it. Pull apart mantle and body (with tentacles). Rinse out and discard contents of mantle. Strip off and discard ink sac and other material that easily separates from body. Pop out horny beaklike mouth from between tentacles; cut out and discard eyes. Chop mantle and body. You should have 1¼ to 1½ cups meat.

In a wide frying pan over medium-high heat, cook onion, garlic, and green pepper in oil until limp. Drain liquid from tomatoes into pan; coarsely chop tomatoes, then add to pan with chervil, basil, salt, rosemary, pepper, and parsley. Reduce heat and simmer, uncovered, stirring occasionally, for about 20 minutes or until slightly thickened. Add squid and simmer until squid is tender (7 to 10 minutes).

Meanwhile, following package directions, cook spaghetti in a large kettle of boiling salted water until al dente; then drain. Arrange spaghetti on a serving dish, ladle sauce over it, and serve. Makes 4 servings.

## CARBONARA

Beaten raw egg is the secret of this delicate and delicious sauce; it coats the spaghetti and causes the bits of cheese and meat to cling evenly. You'll have a showy offering when you assemble carbonara at the table.

¼ pound mild Italian sausage
¼ pound prosciutto or cooked ham, thinly sliced
4 tablespoons butter
½ cup chopped parsley
3 eggs, well beaten
½ cup grated Parmesan cheese
  Freshly ground black pepper
8 ounces spaghetti
  Boiling salted water
  Grated Parmesan cheese

Remove casings from sausages and crumble or chop meat. Finely chop prosciutto. In a wide frying pan over medium-low heat, melt 2 tablespoons of the butter. Add sausage and half the prosciutto to pan and cook, stirring, for about 10 minutes or until sausage is lightly browned and prosciutto is curled. Stir in other half of prosciutto. You can do this ahead and reheat at serving time.

If you wish to complete the preparation at the table, have ready in separate containers the remaining 2 tablespoons butter, parsley, eggs, the ½ cup cheese, and pepper.

Following package directions, cook spaghetti in a large kettle of boiling salted water until al dente; then drain. At the table (if you wish), add spaghetti to hot meat mixture; then add butter and parsley. Mix quickly to blend. At once pour in eggs and quickly lift and mix the spaghetti to coat well with egg. Sprinkle in the ½ cup cheese and a dash of pepper; mix again. Serve with more cheese, if desired. Makes 4 servings.

# HAM & MUSHROOM SPAGHETTI

Here's a family-pleasing spaghetti main dish. It's lightly seasoned, and it has just enough cream to give it a velvet-rich texture. Since this dish doesn't stay hot too long, you might want to start your family on a green salad or fruit salad, then toss the spaghetti with the sauce.

**3 tablespoons butter or margarine**
**½ pound mushrooms, thinly sliced**
**½ pound thinly sliced cooked ham, cut into thin strips**
**¾ cup canned tomato juice**
**½ teaspoon rubbed sage**
**⅛ teaspoon ground nutmeg**
**⅓ cup whipping cream**
**¼ cup chopped parsley**
**½ cup grated Parmesan cheese**
**6 ounces spaghetti or vermicelli Boiling salted water**

In a wide frying pan over medium-high heat, melt butter. Add mushrooms and cook, stirring occasionally, until juices evaporate and mushrooms are lightly browned. Add ham, tomato juice, sage, nutmeg, and cream. Boil, uncovered, over high heat, stirring occasionally, until liquid is reduced to about half (about

8 minutes). Stir in parsley and 1 tablespoon of the cheese.

Following package directions, cook spaghetti in a large kettle of boiling salted water until al dente; then drain. Return spaghetti to kettle, pour sauce over spaghetti, and toss gently. Turn into a serving bowl. Pass remaining cheese at table. Makes 4 servings.

# GREEN CHILE PASTA

This delicious dish is like a Mexican *sopa seca*—"dry soup." Contrary to most rules of pasta cooking that call for lots of boiling water, this pasta cooks in only the amount that it can absorb. The result is a moist, richly flavored pasta. You could enjoy green chile pasta as a main dish with a crisp salad, or serve it as a side dish with plain broiled meat.

**6 strips bacon, diced**
**1 large onion, chopped**
**8 ounces vermicelli or thin spaghetti**
**1 can (about 1 lb.) Italian-style tomatoes**
**1 can (about 14 oz.) beef broth**
**1 can (4 oz.) diced green chiles**
**2 tablespoons red wine vinegar Salt and pepper Grated Parmesan cheese**

In a Dutch oven over medium heat, cook bacon until crisp. Remove bacon with a slotted spoon, drain on paper towels, and set aside. Discard all but ¼ cup of the drippings.

Add onion to drippings and cook, stirring, until limp. Break vermicelli into 2-inch pieces (you should have about 2 cups); stir into onion and continue cooking until onion is golden brown. Add tomatoes and their liquid (break up tomatoes with a spoon), beef broth, chiles, and vinegar; stir well. Cover and simmer until vermicelli is tender and most of the liquid is absorbed (about 15 minutes). Season to taste with salt and pepper.

Turn into a serving dish; top with bacon. Pass cheese at the table. Makes 4 to 6 servings.

# SAFFRON SPAGHETTI BAKE

Pork chops never look more elegant than when served in this colorful cook-ahead dish. Saffron contributes the color. It's very expensive—the most expensive spice in the world, but luckily, a little goes a long way. If you don't want to splurge on saffron, you can use turmeric as a substitute; though it lacks saffron's unique, pleasantly bitter, earthy flavor, turmeric will match the color.

**2 medium-size onions, chopped**
**2 cloves garlic, minced or pressed**
**¼ cup olive oil or salad oil**
**3 medium-size tomatoes, peeled, seeded, and coarsely chopped**
**1 can (4 oz.) diced green chiles, drained**
**1 tablespoon chopped parsley**
**2 beef bouillon cubes**
**¾ teaspoon salt**
**¼ teaspoon saffron or turmeric**
**1 quart boiling water**
**12 ounces spaghetti, broken in half**
**6 garlic sausages (about 1½ lbs.), peeled and sliced**
**6 loin pork chops (about 2 lbs.), cut ¾ inch thick**
**½ cup shredded Cheddar cheese**

In a 4-quart pan over medium heat, cook onions and garlic in 3 tablespoons of the oil until onions are limp. Stir in tomatoes, chiles, parsley, bouillon cubes, salt, saffron, and water. Bring mixture to a boil. Add spaghetti and sausage; reduce heat, cover, and simmer, stirring occasionally, until most of the liquid has been absorbed (about 30 minutes).

Meanwhile, brown chops well on both sides in remaining 1 tablespoon oil. Turn spaghetti mixture into a greased shallow casserole (about 3-quart size). Arrange chops over spaghetti. If made ahead, cool, cover, and refrigerate until next day.

Bake, covered, in a 350° oven for 45 minutes (1 hour if refrigerated) or until chops are tender. Remove cover, sprinkle with cheese, and return to oven for a few minutes until cheese melts. Makes 6 servings.

# TURKEY TETRAZZINI

Luisa Tetrazzini was considered the greatest coloratura of her time, but most people today recognize her name because of a noodle dish.

The brilliant diva was the delight of San Francisco in the early 1900s. There she not only made her American debut, but also gave a memorable Christmas Eve concert on a street corner, singing to a massive audience that had gathered to hear her. She inspired the chef of the Palace Hotel to create the dish named in her honor.

The original version was made with chicken. But the chicken can be replaced by shellfish or turkey with equal bravura.

**6 tablespoons butter or margarine**
**5 tablespoons flour**
**2½ cups chicken broth**
**1¼ cups half-and-half (light cream)**
**½ cup dry white wine**
**¾ cup grated Parmesan cheese**
**¾ pound mushrooms, sliced**
**12 ounces spaghetti**
  **Boiling salted water**
**3 to 4 cups cooked turkey, cut in ½-inch cubes**
  **Salt and white pepper**

In a 2-quart pan, melt 3 tablespoons of the butter over medium heat. Mix in flour and cook, stirring, until bubbly. Remove pan from heat and stir in chicken broth, half-and-half, and wine. Return to heat and cook, stirring, until sauce is smooth and thickened. Stir in Parmesan. Measure out 1 cup of the sauce and reserve both portions.

Melt remaining 3 tablespoons butter in a wide frying pan over medium-high heat. Add mushrooms and cook, stirring, until juices evaporate and mushrooms are lightly browned.

Following package directions, cook spaghetti in a large kettle of boiling salted water until al dente; then drain. Combine spaghetti with the larger portion of sauce, mushrooms (save a few slices for granish), and turkey; mix lightly. Add salt and pepper to taste. Turn into a greased shallow 2-quart casserole or 6 individual casseroles. Spoon the 1 cup reserved sauce evenly over the surface and top with reserved mushroom slices. If made ahead, cool, cover, and refrigerate until next day.

Bake, covered, in a 375° oven for about 45 minutes (1 hour if refrigerated) or until hot and bubbly. Remove cover and broil for a few minutes to brown the top lightly. Makes 6 servings.

# CRAB & SPAGHETTI CASSEROLE

A scene stealer at a party buffet, this casserole has a spunky flavor. Most pasta dishes cool off rather quickly, but this one stays hot for a long time.

**6 ounces spaghetti or vermicelli**
  **Boiling salted water**
**2 tablespoons butter or margarine**
**1 large onion, chopped**
**1 can (10½ oz.) condensed cream of mushroom soup**
**1 cup half-and-half (light cream)**
**1 tablespoon *each* Worcestershire and Dijon mustard**
**½ pound cooked fresh or canned crab**
**2 hard-cooked eggs, diced**
**½ cup thinly sliced water chestnuts**
**1 jar (2 oz.) sliced pimentos, drained**
  **Salt and ground red pepper (cayenne)**
**⅔ cup shredded sharp Cheddar cheese**

Following package directions, cook spaghetti in a large kettle of boiling salted water until al dente; then drain.

Meanwhile, melt butter in a 3-quart pan over medium heat; add onion and cook, stirring occasionally, until limp (about 5 minutes). Stir in soup, then blend in half-and-half, Worcestershire, and mustard. Add spaghetti and mix well. Gently stir in crab, eggs, water chestnuts, and pimentos. Season to taste with salt and red pepper.

Spoon spaghetti mixture into a greased, shallow 2-quart baking dish. Sprinkle evenly with cheese. If made ahead, cover and refrigerate until next day. Bake, uncovered, in a 375° oven for 25 minutes (35 minutes if refrigerated) or until bubbly and heated through. Makes 6 servings.

# TUNA SPAGHETTI PIE

Tuna, cottage cheese, spinach, and Swiss cheese combine with the savory flavors of onion, dill, garlic, and a smidgen of Dijon mustard to form the filling for this unusual pie. "Where's the spaghetti?" you ask. It forms the crust when mixed with Parmesan and eggs.

**6 ounces spaghetti**
  **Boiling salted water**
**2 tablespoons butter or margarine**
**⅓ cup grated Parmesan cheese**
**2 eggs, well beaten**
**1 package (10 or 12 oz.) frozen chopped spinach, thawed**
**2 cans (about 7 oz. *each*) chunk-style tuna, drained and flaked**
**1 medium-size onion, chopped**
**1 cup small curd cream-style cottage cheese**
**1 tablespoon Dijon mustard**
**½ teaspoon *each* dill weed and garlic salt**
**1 cup (4 oz.) shredded Swiss cheese**

Following package directions, cook spaghetti in a large kettle of boiling salted water until al dente; then drain. Combine spaghetti with butter, Parmesan, and eggs; spread over bottom and sides of a well-greased 9-inch pie pan (1½ inches deep).

Press excess liquid out of spinach. Stir together spinach, tuna, onion, cottage cheese, mustard, dill weed, garlic salt, and ½ cup of the Swiss cheese; blend well. Spread in spaghetti-lined pan. If made ahead, cover and refrigerate until next day.

Bake, uncovered, in a 350° oven for 30 minutes (45 minutes if refrigerated) or until set. Sprinkle with remaining cheese and bake for 5 minutes longer or until cheese melts. Makes 6 servings.

# TOMATO BEEF WITH PAN-FRIED NOODLES

It's hard to decide which tastes best, the glazy, succulent meat and vegetable mixture that goes on top, or the crunchy brown noodles below.

¾ pound boneless lean beef
2 teaspoons *each* cornstarch and soy sauce
1 tablespoon *each* dry sherry and water
¼ teaspoon salt
4 tablespoons salad oil
   Cooking sauce (directions follow)
   Pan-fried noodles (directions follow)
½ teaspoon minced fresh ginger
1 clove garlic, minced or pressed
2 large stalks celery, cut in ¼-inch-thick slanting slices
1 medium-size onion, cut in wedges with layers separated
1 green pepper, seeded and cut in 1-inch squares
3 medium-size tomatoes, each cut in 6 wedges

Cut beef with the grain into 1½-inch-wide strips. Cut each strip across the grain in ⅛-inch-thick slanting slices. In a bowl, combine cornstarch, soy, sherry, water, and salt. Add beef and stir to coat, then stir in 1½ teaspoons of the oil; marinate for 15 minutes.

Prepare cooking sauce and set aside. Cook pan-fried noodles; keep warm in a 200° oven.

Heat a wok or wide frying pan over high heat. When pan is hot, add 2 tablespoons of the oil. When oil begins to heat, add ginger and garlic and stir once. Add beef and stir-fry until meat is browned on the outside but still pink within (about 1½ minutes); remove from pan.

Heat remaining 1½ tablespoons oil. Add celery and onion and stir-fry for 1 minute. Add green pepper and stir-fry for 1 minute, adding a few drops of water if pan appears dry. Add tomatoes and stir-fry for 1 minute. Return meat to pan.

Stir cooking sauce, add to pan, and cook, stirring, until sauce bubbles and thickens. To serve, spoon tomato-beef mixture over pan-fried noodles. Makes 4 servings.

**Cooking sauce.** In a bowl, combine 1 tablespoon *each* **soy sauce, Worcestershire,** and **cornstarch;** 3 tablespoons **catsup;** 1 teaspoon **curry powder;** and ½ cup **water.**

**Pan-fried noodles.** Following package directions, cook 1 pound **fresh Chinese noodles** or spaghetti in a large kettle of **boiling salted water** until al dente. Drain, rinse with cold water, and drain again. Stir in 1 tablespoon **sesame oil.**

In a wide frying pan, heat 2 tablespoons **salad oil** over medium-high heat. Spread drained cooked noodles in a layer 1 inch thick (cook in two batches if necessary). Cook until golden brown. Turn noodles over in one piece, add another tablespoon **salad oil,** and brown the other side. Cut in wedges or serve whole, topped with tomato beef.

---

# UDON-SUKI

The Japanese wide noodle, called *udon*, gives its name to this meal-in-one soup that includes meat, vegetables, and noodles.

   Pork balls (directions follow)
6 to 8 cups of cut vegetables (directions follow)
1 dozen fresh clams in the shells
3 packages (about 7 oz. *each*) fresh udon or 6 ounces dry udon or spaghetti
   Boiling salted water
1 tablespoon salad oil
2 cans (46 oz. *each*) chicken broth

Prepare pork balls. Cut and pre-cook vegetables. Scrub clams and rinse in cold water. Arrange meatballs, vegetables, and clams on trays; cover and refrigerate until serving time.

Shortly before serving, cook fresh udon in a large kettle of boiling salted water for 3 minutes or, following package directions, cook spaghetti until al dente. Drain and toss with salad oil.

Before seating guests, heat half the chicken broth until boiling in a cooker at the table; use electric frying pan, or flame-proof casserole set over an alcohol burner. Away from the table, heat remaining chicken broth in a separate pan and keep warm.

At the table, add half the clams to the cooker, cover, and cook until broth resumes boiling; simmer for about 3 minutes. Then add half the meatballs, half of udon, and half of each of the vegetables, or enough for each guest to have a serving. After clams open, spoon some of each ingredient and broth into individual bowls to serve. Then replenish the broth in the cooker and cook the remaining clams, meatballs, udon, and vegetables. Makes 6 servings.

**Pork balls.** In a bowl combine 1 pound **ground lean pork** with 1 **egg,** 2 tablespoons **all-purpose flour,** 1 tablespoon **soy sauce,** and ¼ teaspoon **ground ginger.** Shape into walnut-size balls. Arrange slightly apart in a shallow baking pan. Bake in a 475° oven until browned (about 15 minutes). Save any pan juices to add to broth. Makes about 36 meatballs.

**Vegetables.** Select, cut, and precook any of the following vegetables in **chicken broth** or boiling salted water until just tender; then drain. Cut **carrots** or **celery** in ¼-inch-thick slanting slices and precook for 4 minutes. Cut **cauliflower** or **broccoli** flowerets in ¼-inch slices and precook for 4 minutes. Cut **green onions** in 4-inch lengths and precook for 1 minute. Cut **turnips** or **daikon** (giant white radish) in ¼-inch-thick slices and precook for 3 minutes. Remove ends and strings from **Chinese snow peas** and precook for 1 minute. Slice **fresh mushrooms** through the stems ¼ inch thick; precook for 2 minutes.

---

*Twisty spaghetti, called "fusilli" or "long fusilli," looks ready to wrap itself around your fork. It can replace straight strands in any spaghetti recipe and makes a springy nest for succulent chicken cacciatore (recipe on page 61).*

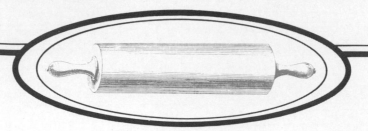

# SELECT A SAUCE

Take your pick—on these two pages there's a sauce for every taste and every shape of pasta. Some recipes yield large quantities that can be frozen in smaller portions and reheated as needed. With a sauce waiting in the freezer, a quick pasta meal is only minutes away.

## TANGY TOMATO SAUCE

*(Pictured on front cover)*

Here's a sauce that is fresh-looking and fresh-tasting. The carrot adds bright color and sweetens the sauce so you don't have to add sugar. This is an excellent sauce for medium-wide or thin noodles, vermicelli, or ricotta-filled pastas.

**1 small onion, finely chopped**
**1 stalk celery, finely chopped**
**1 medium-size carrot, chopped**
**1 clove garlic, minced or pressed**
**6 tablespoons olive oil or salad oil**
**1 can (about 1 lb.) tomatoes**
**1 tablespoon chopped fresh basil leaves or 1 teaspoon dry basil**
**Salt and white pepper**

In a wide frying pan over low heat, cook onion, celery, carrot, and garlic in oil for 15 minutes. Coarsely chop tomatoes, then add to pan with their liquid, as well as basil and salt and pepper to taste. Simmer, covered, for 30 minutes.

Remove about ¾ cup of the sauce and purée it in a food processor or blender; return purée to sauce. Reheat to serve. Makes about 2 cups.

## GREEK MEAT SAUCE

Pickling spices and cinnamon provide an unusual depth of flavor in this aromatic sauce. Use it with Greek dishes, such as pastitsio (page 77), or any time you want a meat sauce with a touch of the exotic. You don't need to save this sauce for Greek dishes, though. It's good tossed with almost any Italian pasta. In fact, it's so good it's worth making in the large quantity this recipe yields. Then you can freeze it in small portions to use for several dishes.

**6 large onions, finely chopped**
**About ½ cup (¼ lb.) butter or margarine**
**6 pounds lean ground beef**
**3 cloves garlic, minced or pressed**
**2 sticks cinnamon**
**1 tablespoon whole mixed pickling spices**
**6 cans (6 oz. *each*) tomato paste**
**2 tablespoons salt**
**Freshly ground pepper**
**1 quart water**

In a wide frying pan, cook onions in 4 tablespoons of the butter over medium-high heat until limp; transfer to a Dutch oven or 8-quart pan. In the frying pan, brown meat in 4 portions, using 1 tablespoon of the butter, as needed, for each portion; add meat to onions. Place garlic, cinnamon sticks, and pickling spices in a cheesecloth bag. Add to meat and onion mixture along with tomato paste, salt, pepper to taste, and water. Cover and simmer, stirring occasionally, for 3 hours or until flavors are blended and sauce has thickened. Makes 4 quarts.

## SAUSAGE TOMATO SAUCE

Hot and mild sausage go together to contribute the spicy taste to this thick, chunky sauce. It's delicious on any medium-size or large pasta, or even on gnocchi.

**2 pounds mild Italian sausages**
**1 pound spicy Italian sausages**
**1 large onion, chopped**
**2 medium-size green peppers, seeded and chopped**
**2 large cans (1 lb. 12 oz. *each*) Italian-style tomatoes**
**2 cans (6 oz. *each*) tomato paste**
**1 teaspoon fennel seeds**

Remove casings from sausages. Crumble meat into a wide frying pan. Cook over medium-high heat until meat is no longer pink. Remove meat from pan, pour off and discard all but 2 tablespoons of the drippings. Add onion and green pepper to pan and cook until onion is limp.

Place meat and onion mixture in a 6-quart kettle or Dutch oven. Add tomatoes and their liquid (break up tomatoes with a spoon), tomato paste, and fennel; stir to blend. Bring mixture to a boil, reduce heat, and simmer, uncovered, stirring occasionally, until sauce is thick (about 3 hours). Makes 1½ quarts.

## QUICK TOMATO MUSHROOM SAUCE

To give this sauce the best consistency, break up the tomatoes thoroughly before adding them to the pan. Use a food processor, blender, or food mill, or use the technique we learned from an Italian chef—crush the tomatoes by squeezing them with your hand.

  6 strips bacon
  ½ pound mushrooms, sliced
  1 clove garlic, minced or pressed
  2 cans (about 1 lb. *each*) Italian-style tomatoes
  1 tablespoon chopped fresh basil or 1½ teaspoons dry
      basil
  ¼ teaspoon pepper
    Salt

In a wide, deep frying pan or Dutch oven over medium-high heat, cook bacon until crisp. Remove from pan, drain on paper towels, then crumble. Pour off and discard all but 3 tablespoons of the drippings. Add mushrooms and garlic to pan and cook, stirring, until mushrooms are lightly browned. Pour tomato liquid into pan. Crush tomatoes and add to pan along with basil and pepper.

Cook, uncovered, over medium-high heat until sauce is thick (about 15 minutes), stirring frequently. Stir in crumbled bacon and add salt if desired. Makes 2½ cups.

## SWISS CHARD SAUCE

If you're looking for a well-flavored meatless sauce, try this one based on five vegetables. The sauce is thick and chunky and best complements a sturdy shape of pasta such as rigatoni, penne, or even gnocchi. Italian-style tomatoes, meatier than regular tomatoes, are definitely best to use here. If you prefer to use regular tomatoes, cook the sauce longer to make it thick.

  3 leeks
  1 large onion, chopped
  ⅓ cup olive oil or salad oil
  ¼ small head cabbage, coarsely chopped
  1 small bunch (about ¾ lb.) Swiss chard, coarsely
      chopped, or 1 box (12 oz.) frozen chopped Swiss
      chard, thawed and drained
  2 cans (about 1 lb. *each*) Italian-style tomatoes
  1 can (8 oz.) tomato sauce
  1 cup chicken broth
  ¾ cup dry white wine
  1½ teaspoons dry basil
  ½ teaspoon *each* salt and thyme leaves
  ¼ teaspoon *each* dry rosemary and pepper

Split leeks in half lengthwise so you can wash them thoroughly, then thinly slice; discard tough green tops. In an 8-quart kettle or Dutch oven, cook leeks and onion in oil over medium-high heat for 5 minutes. Add cabbage and chard and continue cooking, stirring occasionally, until vegetables are soft.

Coarsely chop or crush tomatoes, then add to pan along with their liquid. Stir in tomato sauce, chicken broth, wine, basil, salt, thyme, rosemary, and pepper. Cover and simmer, stirring occasionally, for 1 hour. Uncover and continue cooking until sauce has thickened (about 30 minutes). Makes 6 cups.

## ITALIAN MUSHROOM GRAVY

You can use this classic meatless sauce to dress any kind of pasta—fettuccine, spaghetti, macaroni, even stuffed pasta such as ravioli, tortellini, or cappelletti. You can also use it as the base for a meat sauce, browning ground beef, or cubes of pork or beef, then adding it to the sauce and simmering until tender. Look for dried Italian mushrooms in the gourmet section of your supermarket or in Italian delicatessens or grocery stores.

  1 cup dried Italian mushrooms
  1½ cups warm water
  3 tablespoons olive oil or salad oil
  1½ cups chopped parsley
  2 or 3 stalks celery, chopped
  2 cloves garlic, minced or pressed
  1 2-inch sprig fresh rosemary or ½ teaspoon dry
      rosemary
  2 or 3 leaves fresh thyme or ½ teaspoon dry thyme
      leaves
  5 small leaves fresh sage or ½ teaspoon dry sage
      leaves
  2 cans (about 15 oz. *each*) tomato sauce
  2 cans (about 1 lb. *each*) tomatoes
  ¼ teaspoon crushed red pepper
    Salt to taste

Cover mushrooms with warm water; let stand for 30 minutes.

Heat oil in a wide, deep frying pan or Dutch oven over medium heat. When oil is hot, add parsley, celery, garlic, rosemary, thyme, and sage and cook until vegetables are soft. Stir in tomato sauce, tomatoes and their liquid (break up tomatoes with a spoon), and red pepper. Drain mushrooms; reserve soaking liquid. Chop mushrooms and add to pan along with soaking liquid. Cover and simmer slowly, stirring occasionally, until sauce is thick (about 3 hours). Add salt to taste. Makes about 2½ quarts.

## CHICKEN & SHRIMP NOODLE SALAD

*(Pictured on facing page)*

Chuka soba is the narrow, crinkly, quick-cooking wheat flour noodle that comes in individual packets of Oriental soup mix. Here we've used it not as soup, but as the basis for a refreshing Japanese-style salad. If you can't find chuka soba, you can use strands of spaghetti to make this Oriental dish.

**Sweet-sour dressing
   (directions follow)**
**2 tablespoons sesame seeds**
**4 ounces chuka soba noodles or
   spaghetti**
**Boiling salted water**
**1 tablespoon sesame oil or salad
   oil**
**6 ounces (about 2½ cups) bean
   sprouts**
**1½ cups cooked chicken or ham,
   cut in bite-size pieces**
**1 small cucumber, peeled and
   thinly sliced, or ½ thin-
   skinned cucumber, thinly
   sliced**
**⅓ pound medium-size shrimp,
   cooked, shelled, and
   deveined**
**½ cup sliced green onion**

Prepare salad dressing and set aside. In a small frying pan over low heat, cook sesame seeds until golden (about 2 minutes).

Drop chuka soba noodles in a large kettle of boiling salted water. When water returns to a full boil and noodles float to the top, cook for 2 minutes. (Or, following package directions, cook spaghetti until al dente.) Drain, rinse with cold water, and drain again. Toss noodles with sesame oil; then chill.

Cook bean sprouts in a large kettle of boiling water for 30 seconds. Drain, rinse with cold water, and drain again; chill also.

To serve, place noodles on a

serving plate. Arrange bean sprouts, chicken, cucumber, and shrimp on top of noodles. Sprinkle with green onion and sesame seeds. Drizzle dressing over salad and toss until well blended. Makes 6 servings.

**Sweet-sour dressing.** In a bowl, mix until blended 2 tablespoons **soy sauce,** ⅓ cup **rice wine vinegar** (or 3 tablespoons white wine vinegar), 2 tablespoons **sugar,** ¼ teaspoon **dry mustard,** and a dash of **ground red pepper** (cayenne).

## CHICKEN SOBA

Among the favorite noodles used in Japanese cooking are thin buckwheat strands called *soba.* You can buy dried soba in Oriental markets or you can make your own fresh buckwheat pasta and cut it into thin ribbons. Swimming in bowls of steaming broth, soba makes a satisfying lunch on a cold day.

**4 ounces dried soba or ½ recipe
   buckwheat pasta (page 12),
   cut in thin ribbons**
**Boiling water**
**Cold water**
**6 cups chicken broth**
**2 tablespoons *each* dry sherry
   and soy sauce**
**¼ pound snow peas, ends and
   strings removed**
**1½ to 2 cups shredded cooked
   chicken**
**2 green onions (including tops),
   thinly sliced**

Drop dried soba in a large kettle of boiling water; stir to separate. When water resumes boiling, add ½ cup cold water. Bring to a boil again and cook until soba is al dente (6 to 7 minutes); then drain. Or cook fresh buckwheat noodles in a large kettle of boiling water until al dente (3 to 4 minutes); then drain.

Meanwhile, heat chicken broth, sherry, and soy to simmering in a 2-quart pan. Add snow peas and chicken and cook for 1 minute.

Divide hot noodles among 4 large bowls. Arrange snow peas and chicken on top. Ladle hot broth over noodles. Sprinkle green onion over each serving. Makes 4 servings.

## INDONESIAN BAMIE

Bring out your wok (or use a large frying pan) and invite some friends over to share this marvelous Indonesian dish. First you stir-fry thin strips of flank steak and shrimp in a spicy-hot combination of garlic and crushed red pepper. Then you stir-fry assorted sliced vegetables and add fine strands of cooked vermicelli. It's all ready in a very few minutes.

**8 ounces vermicelli, broken in
   half**
**Boiling salted water**
**5 tablespoons salad oil**
**2 cloves garlic, minced or
   pressed**
**½ teaspoon crushed red pepper**
**1 flank steak (about 1 lb.), cut
   across grain in ⅛-inch-thick
   slices**
**¼ pound raw shrimp, shelled,
   deveined, and cut in half
   lengthwise**
**2 green onions (including tops)
   cut in ½-inch diagonal slices**
**2 cups thinly sliced (about ¼ inch
   thick) cabbage**
**1 cup *each* thinly sliced (about
   ¼ inch thick) leeks and
   celery**
**4 tablespoons soy sauce**

Following package directions, cook vermicelli in a large kettle of boiling salted water until al dente. Drain, rinse with cold water, and drain again; set aside.

Heat a wok or wide frying pan over high heat. When pan is hot, add 2 tablespoons of the oil. When oil begins to heat, add garlic and red pepper and stir once. Add beef and stir-fry for 1 minute. Add shrimp and stir-fry until shrimp are opaque and meat is browned but still pink inside (about 30 seconds). Remove from pan.

Add 2 more tablespoons oil to pan. Add onion, cabbage, leek, and celery slices; stir-fry until vegetables are tender-crisp (about 1½ minutes). Add vermicelli, remaining 1 tablespoon oil, and soy; stir-fry for 1 minute. Return meat mixture to pan and continue stir-frying until most of the liquid has evaporated. Makes 4 to 6 servings.

---

*A refreshing answer for warm-weather menu planning, this Japanese-style chicken and shrimp noodle salad is tossed with a sprightly soy dressing. The recipe is above.*

# Fancy Shapes

## ELBOWS, STARS, CORKSCREWS, SNAILS & MORE

Pasta makes people smile. Just as it's hard to keep a stern and sober face while slurping spaghetti, it's hard to ban humor from the table when everyone's eating butterflies, seashells, small mustaches, feathers, rosary beads, cockscombs, or any of the hundreds of other fancy pasta shapes.

The Italians have a virtual corner on the comedy market when it comes to the commercially made dried pasta featured in this chapter. Though not all the hundreds of shapes enjoyed in Italy are imported for the American market, and even fewer are manufactured by major American pasta companies, you still can find enough pasta shapes in local Italian markets or on supermarket shelves for a month of smiles.

Some pasta shapes come in different colors, like red and green bows. (We think they look best dressed only with butter and Parmesan—so the colors show.) In health food stores you can also find such pasta as artichoke elbows, sesame-corn spirals, and whole wheat shells. Whole-grain pasta takes a little longer to cook and has a stronger flavor, but you can have a good time experimenting with those shapes, too.

Soups, salads, and casseroles are featured in this chapter. Unlike pasta dishes made with fresh fettuccine, which have to be served as soon as they are cooked, most of the dishes can be made in advance, refrigerated or frozen, and then reheated.

The soups are of the hearty, main-dish variety, such as meatball minestrone and Italian sausage soup; they'll fill your kitchen with provocative aromas. The salads range from classic macaroni salad to a curried salmon salad with sunflower seeds. Next comes a veritable casserole bonanza—your idea of macaroni and cheese will never be the same once you've tried the crab and artichoke casserole or the chorizo noodle casserole. For quickly sauced, fancy-shaped pasta, consider serving midsummer pasta or quick conchiglie (small seashells) with basil. Finally, there's a pizza recipe that uses tiny pastina for a crust—it's a winner!

In a recipe's list of ingredients you'll often find two possible pasta shapes given, and then the phrase "or other fancy-shaped pasta." Please feel free to substitute whatever shape catches your fancy. As long as the size is similar to the original, it will work. Check the Pasta Parade glossary at the back of the book for explanations of names and for cooking suggestions.

---

## EASY MINESTRONE

*Minestrone* literally means "big soup." For this recipe, "main-dish soup" would be an accurate translation. Figure it takes just over an hour from the time you brown the ground beef to the moment you ladle the soup into serving bowls. Bread sticks, a crisp salad, a robust red wine, and fruit and cheese for dessert help make a memorable minestrone meal.

**1 pound lean ground beef**
**1 large onion, chopped**
**1 cup chopped celery**
**2 carrots, cut in julienne strips**
**8 cups beef broth**
**½ teaspoon *each* dry basil and**
     **oregano leaves**
**3 ounces wheels, rotelle, or elbow**
     **macaroni**
**1 package (10 or 12 oz.) frozen**
     **chopped spinach, thawed**
**1 can (15 oz.) garbanzo beans**
**½ cup grated Parmesan cheese**
     **Salt and pepper**

In a Dutch oven or 6-quart pan over medium-high heat, brown meat until it loses its pink color. Add onion, celery, and carrots. Cook, stirring occasionally, until vegetables are soft (about 10 minutes). Discard pan drippings. Add beef broth, basil, and oregano. Bring to a boil; then reduce heat and simmer, covered, for 45 minutes.

Add pasta and spinach. Increase heat to medium-high and cook, stirring occasionally, until pasta is al dente (about 10 minutes). Add garbanzos and their liquid and 2 tablespoons of the Parmesan. Heat through. Season to taste with salt and pepper. Pass remaining cheese at the table. Makes 6 to 8 servings.

## MEATBALL MINESTRONE

*(Pictured on page 78)*

Here's a meal-in-a-bowl with some new ideas. You mix ground beef with spinach to make meatballs that jostle corkscrew-shaped noodles, rounds of sliced carrots, beans, and other goodies in a kettle of minestrone. Cheese and crusty bread would round out a country-style supper.

    **1 package (10 or 12 oz.) frozen chopped spinach, thawed**
    **1½ pounds lean ground beef**
    **⅓ cup fine dry bread crumbs**
    **1 egg**
    **1 teaspoon salt**
    **¼ teaspoon pepper**
    **2 tablespoons salad oil**
    **1 large onion, coarsely chopped**
    **7 cups water**
    **7 beef bouillon cubes**
    **1 can (about 1 lb.) tomatoes**
    **1 can (1 lb.) kidney beans**
    **½ teaspoon *each* oregano leaves and dry basil**
    **1 cup *each* sliced carrots and celery**
    **1 cup rotelle or other pasta twists**
    **Grated Parmesan cheese**

With your hands, press out as much water as possible from spinach. Mix together spinach, beef, bread crumbs, egg, salt, and pepper. Shape into 1-inch balls.

Heat oil in a Dutch oven over medium heat. When oil is hot, add a portion of meat balls and brown on all sides. Remove from pan with a slotted spoon, leaving drippings. Repeat until all meatballs are browned. Add onion and cook, stirring occasionally, until limp (about 5 minutes). Stir in water, bouillon cubes, tomatoes and their liquid (break up tomatoes with a spoon), beans and their liquid, oregano, and basil.

Cover and simmer for 10 minutes.

Add carrots and celery; cover and simmer for 10 more minutes. Stir in pasta; cover and simmer for about 10 more minutes or until pasta is al dente. Place meatballs in soup and heat through. Pass Parmesan at the table. Makes 4 to 6 servings.

## ITALIAN SAUSAGE SOUP

Hot and hearty for cool nights, Italian sausage soup is chock-full of all those essential Italian ingredients —zucchini, basil, garlic, tomatoes, and Italian sausage. This is an excellent soup to take on a winter outing or have ready and waiting in the refrigerator to heat and assemble when you return.

    **1½ pounds mild Italian sausages**
    **2 cloves garlic, minced or pressed**
    **2 large onions, chopped**
    **1 large can (1 lb. 12 oz.) Italian-style tomatoes**
    **3 cans (14 oz. *each*) beef broth**
    **1½ cups dry red wine or water**
    **½ teaspoon dry basil**
    **3 tablespoons chopped parsley**
    **1 medium-size green pepper, seeded and chopped**
    **2 medium-size zucchini, cut in ¼-inch-thick slices**
    **5 ounces medium-size bow-shaped noodles (about 3 cups)**
    **Grated Parmesan cheese**

Remove and discard sausage casings; cut sausages in ½-inch lengths. In a 5-quart Dutch oven, cook sausages over medium heat until lightly browned. Spoon off and discard all but 2 tablespoons drippings. Add garlic and onions and cook, stirring occasionally, until limp (about 5 minutes). Stir in tomatoes and their liquid (break up tomatoes with a spoon).

Add broth, wine, and basil. Bring to a boil; then reduce heat and simmer, covered, for 30 minutes. Add parsley, pepper, zucchini, and noodles. Cover and simmer, stirring occasionally, for about 25 minutes or until noodles are al dente. Pass Parmesan at the table. Makes 6 servings.

## PASTA & BEAN SOUP

An Italian specialty, this whole-meal soup draws its hearty flavor from beans, ham, carrots, onion, and tiny pasta. Only at the end of the preparation do you add the distinctive seasoning—a float of lightly cooked minced garlic. Fresh pears, figs, or melon would make a fine finale.

    **2 cups (about 1 lb.) small red beans or cranberry beans**
    **8 cups water**
    **1 clove garlic, minced or pressed**
    **1 large onion, chopped**
    **1½ cups shredded carrots**
    **1 cup finely chopped celery**
    **1 can (about 1 lb.) Italian-style tomatoes**
    **About 3 pounds shank end, bone-in, fully cooked ham**
    **¼ cup pastina, ditalini, or other tiny soup pasta**
    **2 cloves garlic, minced or pressed**
    **2 tablespoons olive oil or salad oil**
    **2 tablespoons minced parsley**
    **Grated Parmesan cheese**

Rinse beans and place in a 6-quart pan with the water. Bring to a rapid boil and continue to boil for 2 minutes. Remove from heat, cover, and let stand for 1 hour.

To pan, add the 1 clove garlic, onion, carrot, celery, tomatoes, and ham. Bring mixture to a boil, reduce heat, and simmer, covered, until beans mash readily (2 to 2½ hours).

Lift out ham and discard bones; coarsely chop ham and set aside. Whirl about half the soup in a blender or food processor until smooth, then return to pan with remaining soup. Add pasta and chopped ham; cook, stirring occasionally, over medium heat for about 5 minutes.

Meanwhile, in a small frying pan over low heat, cook the 2 cloves garlic in oil until golden. Pour soup into a large tureen. Spoon oil and garlic mixture in center of soup and sprinkle parsley around it. Pass Parmesan at the table. Makes 8 to 10 servings.

## CLASSIC MACARONI SALAD

The name says it—this salad is a classic. Take it along on a picnic, serve it at a barbecue, or line it up on a casual party buffet. Classic macaroni salad is a favorite "go-with" . . . it goes with chicken, ribs, hot dogs, hamburgers, as well as more sophisticated fare.

  1 pound salad macaroni or other fancy-shaped pasta
    Boiling salted water
 12 green onions (including tops), thinly sliced
  4 hard-cooked eggs, chopped
  1 cup thinly sliced celery
 12 strips bacon, crisply cooked and crumbled
  1 jar (4 oz.) sliced pimento, drained
  1 cup chopped dill pickle
1½ cups mayonnaise
  1 tablespoons prepared horseradish
  2 teaspoons prepared mustard
  1 tablespoon dill pickle juice
    Salt and pepper

Following package directions, cook macaroni in a large kettle of boiling salted water until al dente. Drain, rinse with cold water, and drain again. Turn into a large bowl and add onion (reserving some green tops for garnish), eggs, celery, bacon, pimento, and pickle.

Combine mayonnaise, horseradish, mustard, and pickle juice; blend well. Stir into pasta mixture; season to taste with salt and pepper and garnish with reserved onion tops. Cover and chill for at least 4 to 6 hours or until next day. Makes 12 to 14 servings.

## MACARONI SALAD WITH VEGETABLE DRESSING

The rich vegetable dressing is a flavorful version of homemade mayonnaise. Made in seconds in a blender or food processor, the mixture can be used as a sauce for lightly cooked spring vegetables, as well as a salad dressing.

  1 pound salad macaroni or other small, fancy-shaped pasta
    Boiling salted water
  1 egg
 ¼ teaspoon salt
 ½ teaspoon prepared mustard
 ¼ cup finely chopped green onion (including tops)
  3 tablespoons *each* finely chopped celery and tarragon vinegar
 ⅛ teaspoon sugar
1¼ cups salad oil
  4 hard-cooked eggs, quartered
  3 or 4 strips bacon, crisply cooked and crumbled

Following package directions, cook macaroni in a large kettle of boiling salted water until al dente. Drain, rinse with cold water, and drain again. Turn into a large bowl.

In a blender or food processor, put egg, salt, mustard, onion, celery, vinegar, and sugar. Cover and whirl until smooth. With motor still running, *very slowly* add oil, blending until thickened. Pour over cooked pasta and toss gently. Cover and chill for 4 hours or until next day. Garnish with eggs and bacon. Makes 8 to 10 servings.

## QUICK ARTICHOKE PASTA SALAD

Artichoke marinade acts like the genie in the jar for this recipe, granting your wish for an instant, well-seasoned salad dressing. All you have to do is combine the marinated artichokes with mushrooms, tomatoes, and ripe olives and—presto—you've composed the perfectly dressed pasta salad.

  4 ounces salad macaroni
    Boiling salted water
  1 jar (6 oz.) marinated artichoke hearts
 ¼ pound whole small mushrooms
  2 medium-size tomatoes, seeded and cut into bite-size pieces
  1 cup medium-size pitted ripe olives
    Salt and pepper

Following package directions, cook macaroni in a large kettle of boiling salted water until al dente. Drain, rinse with cold water, and drain again. Turn into a large bowl.

Combine artichokes and their liquid, mushrooms, tomatoes, and olives. Add mixture to cooked pasta and toss gently. Cover and refrigerate for at least 4 hours or until next day. Before serving, season with salt and pepper to taste. Makes 4 to 6 servings.

## CAPPELLETTI PESTO SALAD

*(Pictured on facing page)*

That versatile basil and Parmesan sauce, pesto, turns up decorating hats in this recipe. But the little hats (cappelletti) are not the filled kind you can make at home. These are dried packaged pasta, like macaroni. Perhaps we should revise the old Yankee Doodle ditty and sing, "Stick some basil on a hat and call it cappelletti."

 ⅓ cup pesto sauce (page 21)
  8 ounces cappelletti or other medium-size fancy-shaped pasta
    Boiling salted water
 ⅓ cup olive oil
  2 tablespoons white wine vinegar
  1 small clove garlic, minced or pressed

Prepare pesto sauce; set aside.

Following package directions, cook cappelletti in a large kettle of boiling salted water until al dente. Drain, rinse with cold water, and drain again. Turn into a large bowl.

Stir together pesto sauce, oil, vinegar, and garlic; pour over cooked pasta and toss gently. Chill for at least 1 hour or until next day. Makes 4 to 6 servings.

*A spunky change* from plain macaroni salad, cappelletti pesto salad (recipe above) makes a quick luncheon when served with cold cuts. Pesto—that divine combination of fresh basil and Parmesan—is reinforced with garlic and thinned with olive oil to dress the hat-shaped cappelletti.

## CURRIED SALMON SALAD

Sunflower seeds, crunchy vegetables, and a lively curry dressing blend in a medley of tastes and textures.

**Curry dressing (recipe follows)**
**12 ounces conchiglie or other small shell-shaped pasta**
**Boiling salted water**
**½ cup *each* salted shelled sunflower seeds, finely chopped green pepper, and thinly sliced green onions (including tops)**
**1 cup chopped celery**
**1 package (10 oz.) frozen peas, thawed and drained**
**2 cups cooked salmon or 2 cans (about 7 oz. *each*) salmon**
**Parsley sprigs**
**3 hard-cooked eggs, thinly sliced**

Prepare curry dressing; set aside.

Following package directions, cook conchiglie in a large kettle of boiling salted water until al dente. Drain, rinse with cold water, and drain again. Turn into a large bowl. Add sunflower seeds, green pepper, onions, celery, and peas; then add dressing and toss gently. Cover; chill for at least 3 hours or until next day.

To serve, spoon pasta salad onto a large platter; flake salmon (if using canned salmon, first drain and remove skin and bones) into the center and garnish with parsley sprigs and egg slices. Makes 6 to 8 servings.

**Curry dressing.** In a bowl, stir together ¾ cup **mayonnaise,** 1½ tablespoons *each* **curry powder** and **prepared mustard,** ¼ cup **lemon juice,** and 5 cloves **garlic** (minced or pressed) until well blended; then stir in 2 cups (8 oz.) shredded **sharp Cheddar cheese.**

## CHICKEN SALAD WITH PASTA TWISTS

In this salad, rotelle are combined with spinach, chicken, and a sweet-sour dressing to make a salad with an Oriental accent.

**6 ounces rotelle or other pasta twists**
**Boiling salted water**
**¼ cup sesame seeds**
**½ cup salad oil**
**⅓ cup *each* soy sauce and white wine vinegar**
**3 tablespoons sugar**
**½ teaspoon salt**
**¼ teaspoon pepper**
**3 cups cold shredded cooked chicken**
**½ cup *each* chopped parsley and thinly sliced green onion (including tops)**
**8 cups lightly packed torn spinach leaves**

Following package directions, cook rotelle in a large kettle of boiling salted water until al dente. Drain, rinse with cold water, and drain again. Turn into a large bowl.

In a small frying pan, combine sesame seeds and ¼ cup of the oil; cook over medium-low heat, stirring occasionally, until seeds are golden (about 2 minutes). Let cool. Stir in remaining oil, soy, vinegar, sugar, salt, and pepper. Pour over cooked pasta, add chicken, and toss gently. Cover and chill for at least 2 hours or until next day.

To serve, add parsley, onion, and spinach; toss lightly. Makes 6 to 8 servings.

## EASY MACARONI & SAUSAGE BAKE

After you've browned the sausage, you're only a half-hour away from sitting down to eat this macaroni and sausage bake.

**1½ pounds mild or spicy Italian-style sausages**
**6 ounces lumache, wheels, or other medium-size pasta**
**Boiling salted water**
**1 cup (4 oz.) shredded Cheddar cheese**
**1 teaspoon *each* oregano leaves and dry basil**
**½ teaspoon *each* salt and pepper**
**Dash of ground red pepper (cayenne)**
**1 package (10 oz.) frozen peas, thawed**
**½ cup milk**

Remove and discard sausage casings. Crumble sausage into a wide frying pan and cook over medium heat until browned (about 6 minutes). Drain and set aside.

Following package directions, cook pasta in a large kettle of boiling salted water until al dente, then drain. Turn into a large bowl and add sausage, ¾ cup of the cheese, oregano, basil, salt, pepper, red pepper, peas, and milk. Toss lightly to blend ingredients, then turn into a shallow, greased 2½-quart baking dish and sprinkle with remaining cheese. If made ahead, cover and refrigerate until next day.

Bake, covered, in a 350° oven for 20 minutes, then uncover and bake for 10 to 15 minutes longer or until bubbly. Makes 6 servings.

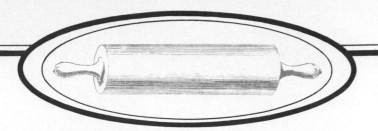

# How Much Pasta to Cook

Watching a boiling vat of pasta expand to a quantity suitable for the entire city of Naples—like watching too much soap bubbling out of the clothes washer—is one of those all too familiar scenes from Life's Daily Comedy.

To figure how much pasta to cook, use this general guideline: 2 ounces packaged dried pasta makes about 1 cup cooked pasta. This is only a rough estimate, though, because spaghetti and macaroni products approximately double in volume after cooking, but packaged egg noodles don't expand quite that much.

If you use the dough recipes in this book to make homemade pasta, figure on one recipe making about 4 cups cooked pasta. The quantity will vary somewhat with the type of flour, the duration of kneading, and the thickness to which the pasta is rolled. Four cups pasta should make 4 to 6 servings, depending on the amount of sauce used and whether you serve it as a side dish, main dish, or separate course. Because most of the dough recipes are based on 2 cups flour and 2 eggs, you can divide them easily to make smaller quantities.

## How to Figure Pasta Quantities

|  | Weight (uncooked) | Quantity (cooked) |
|---|---|---|
| **Packaged dried pasta:** | | |
| Egg noodles | 8 ounces | 4 cups |
| Spaghetti | 8 ounces | 4–5 cups |
| Elbow Macaroni | 8 ounces | 4–4½ cups |
| **Homemade pasta:** | | |
| Medium-wide and thin noodles | 12–14 ounces | 4 cups |

## Red Hot Macaroni & Cheese

Where is it written that because a dish is meatless it has to be boring? Zap those taste buds awake with this red hot macaroni and cheese.

**1 pound medium-size elbow macaroni**
**Boiling salted water**
**⅓ cup butter or margarine**
**1 medium-size onion, finely chopped**
**½ cup finely chopped celery**
**⅓ cup all-purpose flour**
**2¼ cups milk**
**1 cup whipping cream**
**1 teaspoon *each* crushed red pepper and Worcestershire**
**4 cups (1 lb.) shredded sharp Cheddar cheese**
**½ cup dry white wine**
**Salt and pepper**
**1 red bell pepper, cut into rings**

Following package directions, cook macaroni in a large kettle of boiling salted water until al dente, then drain and set aside.

Meanwhile, melt butter in a wide frying pan over medium heat. Add onion and celery and cook, stirring occasionally, until tender (about 5 minutes). Stir in flour and cook for 1 minute. Remove pan from heat and gradually stir in milk and cream. Return pan to heat and cook, stirring constantly, until smooth and thick.

Reduce heat and add red pepper, Worcestershire, and 3 cups of the cheese. Stir until cheese melts; add wine. Combine cooked macaroni and cheese sauce; add salt and pepper to taste. Turn into a shallow 3-quart baking dish; arrange bell pepper rings on top, then sprinkle with remaining cheese. If made ahead, cover and refrigerate until next day.

Bake, uncovered, in a 375° oven for 25 to 35 minutes or until bubbly and lightly browned. Makes 8 to 10 servings.

## Pastitsio

This delicious Greek casserole is a fine choice to feature for a company buffet.

**4 cups Greek meat sauce (page 68)**
**14 ounces mostaccioli or other medium-size fancy-shaped pasta**
**Boiling salted water**
**2 tablespoons *each* butter and all-purpose flour**
**3 cups milk**
**½ teaspoon salt**
**Freshly ground pepper**
**6 eggs**
**2 cups (6 oz.) grated Romano cheese**
**¼ teaspoon ground cinnamon**

*(Continued on page 79)*

Prepare Greek meat sauce.

Following package directions, cook mostaccioli in a large kettle of boiling salted water until al dente. Drain, rinse with cold water, and drain again.

Melt butter in a large pan over medium heat. Blend in flour and cook, stirring, until bubbly. Remove pan from heat and gradually stir in milk. Return pan to heat and cook, stirring constantly, until sauce is smooth and thickened. Add salt and pepper. Beat eggs until well mixed; then stir hot white sauce slowly into beaten eggs to make a custard sauce.

Spoon ⅓ of the pasta into a buttered 9 by 13-inch baking pan at least 2 inches deep. Cover with 2 cups meat sauce and sprinkle generously with some of the cheese; dust with ⅛ teaspoon of the cinnamon. Cover with another ⅓ of the pasta and spoon over remaining meat sauce. Sprinkle generously with cheese and top with remaining pasta.

Pour custard sauce over pasta and poke pasta with a fork in many places to let sauce run to bottom of pan. Dust top lightly with remaining cinnamon and remaining cheese. If made ahead, cool, cover, and refrigerate until next day.

Bake in a 350° oven for 40 to 50 minutes or until custard is set and top is lightly browned. Let cool slightly, then cut into squares. Makes 8 to 10 servings.

---

# CHORIZO NOODLE CASSEROLE

Spicy Mexican chorizo sausage, green chiles, and jack cheese combine for an anything-but-bland variation on the macaroni and cheese

---

*Corkscrew-shaped rotelle, meatballs made with spinach and beef, and chunks of vegetables jostle in this hearty meatball minestrone (recipe on page 73). It's the perfect main-dish soup for chilly evenings.*

theme. You can assemble this main-dish casserole in the morning, refrigerate it, then heat it before serving.

**12 ounces rotelle or other pasta twists**
 **Boiling salted water**
**1 tablespoon butter or margarine**
**4 medium-size (about 3½ oz. *each*) chorizo sausages**
**1 small onion, coarsely chopped**
**1 canned green chile (part of a 4 oz. can), chopped**
**1 cup milk**
**½ teaspoon salt**
 **Dash of pepper**
**2 cups (8 oz.) shredded jack cheese**
**6 to 8 tomato slices**

Following package directions, cook rotelle in a large kettle of boiling salted water until al dente. Drain, rinse with cold water, and drain again.

Meanwhile, melt butter in a wide frying pan over medium-high heat. Remove sausage casings, crumble meat into pan, add onion, and cook until sausage is browned and onion is limp (about 5 minutes). Pour off drippings and add cooked pasta, chile, milk, salt, and pepper to taste.

Pour half the mixture into a greased 2½-quart casserole; sprinkle with half the cheese. Add remaining mixture, arrange tomato slices on top, and sprinkle with remaining cheese. If made ahead, cover and refrigerate until next day.

Bake, uncovered, in a 350° oven for 25 to 35 minutes or until top is slightly browned. Makes 6 servings.

---

# HERBED TUNA CASSEROLE

Everyone's kitchen repertoire includes a tuna-noodle casserole, usually served when the cook runs out of ideas. While still a convenience casserole, this variation on the tuna-noodle theme is full of fresh tastes. Dill and celery seed perk up the flavor, a little sherry adds a touch of class, and shell-shaped pasta in place of the usual noodles or macaroni gives the dish a whole new look.

**6 ounces medium-size conchiglie or other fancy-shaped pasta**
 **Boiling salted water**
**2 cans (about 7 oz. *each*) chunk-style tuna, drained**
**1 package (10 oz.) frozen peas, thawed**
**½ pound mushrooms, sliced and sautéed in 2 tablespoons butter (optional)**
**½ teaspoon garlic salt**
**¼ teaspoon *each* dill weed and celery seed**
**⅛ teaspoon pepper**
**2 cans (10½ oz. *each*) cream of mushroom soup**
**¼ cup milk**
**3 tablespoons dry sherry**
**½ cup soft bread crumbs**
**2 tablespoons butter or margarine, melted**

Following package directions, cook conchiglie in a large kettle of boiling salted water until al dente; then drain.

Grease a 2½-quart casserole and arrange tuna from 1 of the cans in the bottom. In a bowl, combine peas, mushrooms (if used), garlic salt, dill weed, celery seed, and pepper. Spread half the mixture over tuna.

In another bowl, combine mushroom soup, milk, and sherry; pour half of it over pea mixture, then top with noodles. Add tuna from second can, then remaining pea mixture, and remaining soup mixture. Combine bread crumbs and melted butter; sprinkle over top. If made ahead, cover and refrigerate until next day.

Bake, uncovered, in a 350° oven for 30 to 35 minutes or until bubbly and lightly browned. Makes 6 servings.

---

# CRAB & ARTICHOKE CASSEROLE

Every once in a while you come across a dish that really sings to your taste buds. This easily assembled casserole is one of those. Artichoke hearts, crab, and Swiss cheese harmonize with bow-shaped pasta. White wine, a dash of Worcestershire, and a sprinkling of Parmesan underscore the main flavors.

*(Continued on next page)*

**6 ounces bow-shaped pasta or
   other medium-size fancy-
   shaped pasta**
   **Boiling salted water**
**3 tablespoons butter or
   margarine**
**3 tablespoons all-purpose flour**
**1 cup milk**
**½ cup dry white wine or chicken
   broth**
**½ cup shredded Swiss cheese**
**2 teaspoons Worcestershire**
**2 packages (9 oz. *each*) frozen
   artichoke hearts, cooked and
   drained**
**¾ pound cooked fresh or canned
   crab**
**2 tablespoons grated Parmesan
   cheese**

Following package directions, cook pasta in a large kettle of boiling salted water until al dente; then drain.

Meanwhile, melt butter in a small pan over medium heat. Blend in flour and cook, stirring, until bubbly. Remove pan from heat and gradually stir in milk. Return to heat and cook, stirring constantly, until smooth and thickened. Slowly blend in wine, Swiss cheese, and Worcestershire; cook just until cheese melts.

Spoon a thin layer of sauce into a 2½-quart casserole. Arrange half the artichokes (reserve a few for garnish), crab, and pasta in even

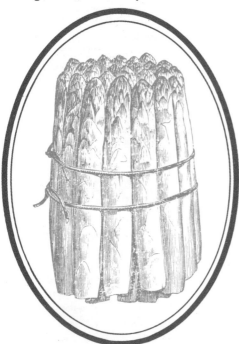

layers over the sauce. Cover with half the sauce. Repeat this layering, ending with sauce. Sprinkle Parmesan over sauce. If made ahead, cover and refrigerate until next day.

Bake, uncovered, in a 350° oven for 30 to 35 minutes or until hot. Garnish with remaining artichokes before serving. Makes 6 servings.

## SEAFOOD ROTELLE RAMEKINS

Mellow, creamy sauce surrounds mushrooms, shrimp, and short corkscrew-shaped noodles. Special enough for an intimate dinner by candlelight, these individual casseroles take remarkably little time to assemble and cook.

**¼ cup butter or margarine**
**½ cup thinly sliced green onions
   (including tops)**
**3 tablespoons all-purpose flour**
**1 cup chicken broth**
**½ cup bottled clam juice**
**¼ cup *each* dry white wine and
   whipping cream**
**¼ teaspoon oregano leaves**
**½ cup grated Parmesan or
   shredded Swiss cheese**
**1 clove garlic, minced or pressed**
**¼ pound mushrooms, sliced**
**4 ounces rotelle**
   **Boiling salted water**
**¾ pound small, cooked shrimp**

Melt 2 tablespoons of the butter in a small pan over medium heat; add onions and cook, stirring occasionally, until limp (about 4 minutes). Blend in flour and cook, stirring, until bubbly. Remove pan from heat and stir in chicken broth, clam juice, wine, cream, and oregano. Return pan to heat and cook, stirring constantly, until sauce is smooth and thickened. Stir in half the cheese; set aside.

In a wide frying pan over medium heat, melt remaining 2 tablespoons butter. Add garlic and mushrooms and cook just until mushrooms are limp (about 4 minutes).

Following package directions, cook pasta in a large kettle of boiling salted water until al dente; then

drain. Combine sauce, mushroom mixture, rotelle, and shrimp (reserve a few for garnish). Pour into 4 buttered ramekins (about 2-cup size). Top with reserved shrimp and sprinkle with remaining cheese. If made ahead, cover and refrigerate until next day.

Bake, uncovered, in a 375° oven for 10 to 15 minutes or until hot and bubbly. Broil top until lightly browned, if desired. Makes 4 servings.

## CRAB GIOVANNI

Leave your guests purring happily—serve them this delightful crab casserole. Seashell pasta and crab are baked in a mélange of vegetables, stuffed green olives, cheese, sour cream, and tomatoes.

**¼ cup butter or margarine**
**2 medium-size onions, coarsely
   chopped**
**¼ pound mushrooms, sliced**
**1 clove garlic, minced or pressed**
**6 ounces medium-size conchiglie**
   **Boiling salted water**
**¾ pound cooked fresh or canned
   crab**
**¼ cup sliced stuffed green olives**
**1 cup (4 oz.) shredded sharp
   Cheddar cheese**
**¼ cup sour cream**
**1 can (about 1 lb.) tomatoes**
**¾ teaspoon salt**
**½ teaspoon dry basil**

In a wide frying pan over medium heat, melt butter. Add onions, mushrooms, and garlic and cook until onions are limp (about 5 minutes). Following package directions, cook pasta in a large kettle of boiling salted water until al dente; drain and combine with onion-mushroom mixture. Add crab, olives, cheese, sour cream, tomatoes and their liquid (break up tomatoes with a spoon), salt, and basil.

Pour mixture into a greased 1½-quart baking dish. If made ahead, cover and refrigerate until next day. Bake, uncovered, in a 350° oven for 30 to 35 minutes or until hot and bubbly. Makes 4 to 6 servings.

# HAM & PEA RAMEKINS

These individual casseroles, containing a fancied-up version of macaroni and cheese, would be tasty at a brunch. If you're cooking just for yourself, you can freeze the ramekins and heat them as needed.

- ¼ cup sliced almonds
- ¼ cup butter or margarine
- ¼ pound mushrooms, thinly sliced
- ¼ pound cooked ham, cut into thin strips
- 1 package (10 oz.) frozen tiny peas, thawed
- 2 tablespoons all-purpose flour
- 1½ cups *each* milk and half-and-half (light cream)
- 1 cup (4 oz.) shredded Swiss cheese
- 12 ounces mostaccioli or other medium-size fancy-shaped pasta
- Boiling salted water

Spread almonds in a shallow pan and toast in a 350° oven until lightly browned (about 8 minutes).

In a wide frying pan over medium heat, melt 2 tablespoons of the butter. Add mushrooms and cook until limp (about 5 minutes). Add ham and continue to cook until most of the mushroom liquid has evaporated. Remove from heat and add peas; set aside.

In a 2-quart pan over medium heat, melt remaining 2 tablespoons butter. Blend in flour and cook, stirring, until bubbly. Remove pan from heat and gradually stir in milk and half-and-half. Return pan to heat and cook, stirring constantly, until sauce is smooth and thickened. Stir in cheese and remove from heat.

Following package directions, cook mostaccioli in a large kettle of boiling salted water until al dente. Drain and spoon into 6 buttered ramekins (about 2-cup size). Top each with an equal amount of mushroom mixture, stirring slightly to mix ingredients. Spoon an equal amount of cheese sauce over each and distribute almonds equally over cheese sauce; cover lightly with foil. If made ahead, refrigerate until next day.

Bake in a 350° oven for 12 to 15 minutes or until heated through. Makes 6 servings.

# SICILIAN BEEF & VEGETABLE CASSEROLE

This richly seasoned casserole has three preparation stages. First you make the meat sauce and let it simmer while you cook the pasta and combine it with the spinach. Then you layer both the sauce and the pasta with cheese and bake it.

- 1 tablespoon salad oil
- 1½ pounds lean ground beef
- 4 medium-size carrots, diced
- 1 large onion, chopped
- ¼ pound mushrooms, sliced
- 2 cans (6 oz. *each*) tomato paste
- 1 can (about 1 lb.) tomatoes
- ⅔ cup dry sherry or water
- 1½ teaspoons *each* salt, sugar, dry basil, and oregano leaves
- ½ teaspoon *each* pepper and garlic powder
- 6 ounces elbow macaroni or other medium-size fancy-shaped pasta
- Boiling salted water
- 1 package (10 or 12 oz.) frozen chopped spinach, thawed and drained
- 1½ cups (6 oz.) shredded Cheddar cheese

In a wide frying pan over medium heat, add oil. When oil is hot, add beef and cook until browned and crumbly. Remove with a slotted spoon and transfer to a Dutch oven or 3-quart pan.

To pan drippings, add carrots, onion, and mushrooms; cook, stirring occasionally, for 5 minutes. Add to meat along with tomato paste, tomatoes and their liquid (break up tomatoes with a spoon), sherry, salt, sugar, basil, oregano, pepper, and garlic powder. Reduce heat and simmer, uncovered, for 30 minutes.

Meanwhile, following package directions, cook pasta in a large kettle of boiling salted water until al dente; drain and combine with spinach. Place half the pasta mixture in a greased 9 by 13-inch baking pan; top with half the meat sauce and ½ cup of the cheese. Repeat layers, sprinkling remaining 1 cup cheese on top. If made ahead, cover and refrigerate until next day.

Bake, uncovered, in a 375° oven for 30 to 40 minutes or until heated through. Makes 6 to 8 servings.

# ROTELLE WITH TOMATO SAUCE

A robust, garlic-and-onion-flavored tomato sauce made with pure butter and olive oil dresses corkscrew-shaped noodles. You can make the sauce ahead of time and refrigerate or freeze it, then assemble the dish when you need a quick, fuss-free supper. An antipasto plate of cheese and cold cuts would go well with this dish.

- ¼ cup *each* olive oil and butter or margarine
- 3 whole cloves garlic, peeled
- 1 large onion, thinly sliced and separated into rings
- 5 large tomatoes, peeled, seeded, and chopped
- 1½ teaspoons salt
- ¼ teaspoon pepper
- 1 teaspoon oregano leaves
- 8 ounces rotelle or other spiral-shaped pasta
- Boiling salted water
- Grated Parmesan cheese
- ¼ pound mushrooms, sliced and sautéed in 2 tablespoons butter (optional)

Heat oil and butter in a wide frying pan over medium heat. Add garlic and onion; cook, stirring occasionally, until onion is limp. Remove garlic and add tomatoes, salt, pepper, and oregano; bring to a boil. Reduce heat, cover, and simmer, stirring occasionally, until sauce has thickened (about 1 hour).

Following package directions, cook rotelle in a large kettle of boiling salted water until al dente. Drain and turn onto a deep platter. Spoon tomato sauce over rotelle, sprinkle with Parmesan, and top with sautéed mushrooms, if desired. Makes 4 servings.

### PASTA WHEELS WITH SAUSAGE & TOMATOES

You won't have any trouble rounding up the family for dinner when you serve this dish. The heady aroma of Italian sausage, onion, and garlic simmering with tomatoes will lure everyone right into the kitchen, forks poised. Fortunately, the mouthwatering sausage sauce has to simmer for only 15 minutes before you stir in cooked wheel-shaped pasta and set the delicious casserole on the table. You might want to follow this hearty entrée with a fresh pineapple salad.

1 pound mild Italian sausages
1 medium-size onion, coarsely chopped
1 clove garlic, minced, or pressed
1 can (about 1 lb.) Italian-style tomatoes
1 teaspoon oregano leaves
¼ teaspoon *each* thyme leaves and pepper
2 tablespoons *each* minced parsley and catsup
12 ounces wheels or other medium-size fancy-shaped pasta
Boiling salted water
Chopped parsley
Grated Parmesan cheese

Remove and discard sausage casings; slice sausages diagonally into ½-inch-thick pieces. In a wide frying pan over medium-high heat, cook sausages until browned (about 5 minutes). Add onion and garlic and continue to cook, stirring occasionally, for about 3 minutes or until onion is limp. Add tomatoes and their liquid (break up tomatoes with a spoon). Stir in oregano, thyme, pepper, parsley, and catsup. Simmer, uncovered, for about 15 minutes or until sauce is slightly thickened and reduced to about 3½ cups.

Following package directions, cook pasta in a large kettle of boiling salted water until al dente; drain. Stir hot pasta into sauce and turn onto a platter. Garnish with chopped parsley and pass Parmesan at the table. Makes 4 to 6 servings.

### RIGATONI WITH EGGPLANT SAUCE

A bold sauce for a bold pasta shape, the eggplant mixture includes garlic, onions, olives, pimento, and anchovy paste. This excellent meatless main dish would go well with a romaine salad, and ambrosia for dessert.

¼ cup olive oil or salad oil
1 small eggplant (about ¾ lb.), peeled and cut into ¾-inch cubes
1 large onion, coarsely chopped
1 large clove garlic, minced or pressed
1 small green pepper, seeded and cut into thin strips
1 can (about 1 lb.) Italian-style tomatoes
1 teaspoon sugar
1½ teaspoons dry basil
2 teaspoons anchovy paste
2 tablespoons chopped parsley
1 can (2¼ oz.) sliced ripe olives
1 jar (2 oz.) sliced pimento, drained
Salt and pepper
10 ounces rigatoni or medium-size shell-shaped pasta
Boiling salted water
½ cup grated Parmesan cheese

Heat oil in a Dutch oven or 3-quart pan over medium heat; add eggplant and onion and cook, stirring occasionally, until eggplant is very soft and lightly browned (about 25 minutes). Add garlic and green pepper and cook, uncovered, for 2 minutes.

Add tomatoes and their liquid (break up tomatoes with a spoon), sugar, basil, and anchovy paste. Cover, reduce heat, and simmer, stirring occasionally, for 15 minutes. Add parsley, olives, and pimento. Simmer, uncovered, stirring occasionally, until sauce is thick (about 20 minutes). Add salt and pepper to taste.

Following package directions, cook pasta in a large kettle of boiling salted water until al dente. Drain and turn into a deep platter. Spoon eggplant sauce over pasta and sprinkle with 2 tablespoons of the Parmesan. Pass remaining Parmesan at the table. Makes 6 servings.

### CRESTE DI GALLI WITH CREAMY SWISS CHARD SAUCE

Vegetable side dish and pasta side dish combine in this recipe. If you can't find creste di galli (cockscombs), use mostaccioli—the thick, rich vegetable sauce goes best on a hefty noodle.

6 cups shredded Swiss chard or 3 packages (10 oz. *each*) frozen chopped Swiss chard
6 tablespoons butter or margarine
2 large onions, chopped
4 cloves garlic, minced or pressed
2 teaspoons all-purpose flour
¾ teaspoon *each* dry basil and ground nutmeg
1 large package (8 oz.) cream cheese
1½ cups half-and-half (light cream)
1 pound creste di galli, mostaccioli, or other medium-size fancy-shaped pasta
Boiling salted water
3 strips bacon, crisply cooked and crumbled
⅓ cup pine nuts
Grated Parmesan cheese

In a wide frying pan over medium heat, cook fresh chard. Cover with boiling salted water, bring to a boil, and cook until just tender (3 to 5 minutes). Drain chard. If using frozen chard, just thaw and drain.

Melt 4 tablespoons of the butter in the frying pan; add onions and garlic and cook, stirring often, until onion is limp (about 5 minutes). Blend in flour, basil, nutmeg, and cream cheese until cheese melts. Remove pan from heat and gradually stir in cream. Return pan to heat and cook, stirring constantly, until sauce is smooth and thickened. Just before serving, stir in chard and cook until heated through.

Following package directions, cook pasta in a large kettle of boiling salted water until al dente. Drain and turn onto a large platter. Spoon sauce over pasta and top with bacon and nuts. Pass Parmesan at the table. Makes 6 to 8 servings.

# PASTINA PIZZA

Pastina are tiny pasta. They come in dozens of shapes, from miniature elbow macaroni to stars. Though pastina usually appear in soup, you can use them to form a crust for an unusal pizza. We like the chewy texture of whole wheat pastina for the crust, but regular pastina works, too. You can be restrained and use just one topping, or go for the works. Feel free to add to the toppings at the end of the recipe.

**5 ounces (1 cup) whole wheat, spinach, or regular pastina**
**Boiling salted water**
**1 cup (4 oz.) shredded Cheddar cheese**
**¼ cup finely chopped onion**
**1 egg, lightly beaten**
**1 can (1 lb.) tomato purée**
**1 teaspoon *each* oregano leaves and dry basil**
**½ teaspoon garlic powder**
**8 to 12 ounces shredded mozzarella cheese**
**Toppings (suggestions follow)**

Following package directions, cook pastina in a large kettle of boiling salted water until al dente. Drain; then combine with Cheddar, onion, and egg. Using a spatula, press mixture evenly into a greased 12 to 14-inch pizza pan. Bake in a 350° oven for 30 to 35 minutes or until firm when touched.

Meanwhile, combine tomato purée, oregano, basil, and garlic powder. Spoon sauce onto crust, spreading evenly to outer edges. Add one or more toppings and sprinkle with mozzarella. Return to 350° oven and bake for 10 to 12 minutes or until cheese is melted. Cut into wedges to serve. Makes 6 servings.

**Toppings.** Choose from the following: ½ pound **mushrooms** (sliced and sautéed in 2 tablespoons butter) 2 cans (about 2 oz. *each*) sliced **ripe olives,** 1 **green pepper** (cut into rings), ¼ pound sliced **salami** or **pepperoni,** ¼ to ½ pound cooked **ground beef** or cooked **mild sausage,** 1 large **tomato** (thinly sliced).

# QUICK CONCHIGLIE WITH BASIL

This spicy basil sauce heats while the pasta shells cook; then you simply drain the pasta and spoon the sauce over each serving.

**8 ounces conchiglie or other medium-size shell-shaped pasta**
**Boiling salted water**
**¼ cup minced fresh basil (or 2 tablespoons dry basil)**
**2 tablespoons minced parsley**
**1 clove garlic, minced or pressed**
**1 tablespoon melted butter**
**¼ cup olive oil or salad oil**
**2 tablespoons grated Parmesan cheese**
**½ teaspoon *each* salt and ground nutmeg**
**Dash of chile powder**
**½ cup hot water**
**Freshly ground black pepper**
**Grated Parmesan cheese**

Following package directions, cook pasta in a large kettle of boiling salted water until al dente.

Meanwhile, in a pan, combine basil, parsley, garlic, butter, oil, Parmesan, salt, nutmeg, chile, and hot water; heat mixture over low heat until you drain the pasta. Turn cooked pasta onto a deep platter, spoon over sauce, and sprinkle with pepper and more Parmesan to taste. Makes 4 to 6 servings.

# SHRIMP CONCHIGLIE

Following the Northern Italian tradition that eschews tomato sauce, shrimp conchiglie is a delicately sauced combination of seafood and seashell pasta.

**12 ounces conchiglie or other medium-size shell-shaped pasta**
**Boiling salted water**
**¾ cup butter**
**1½ teaspoons dry basil**
**1 tablespoon minced parsley**
**¾ pound small cooked shrimp**
**1 teaspoon dry sherry**
**Salt**
**Grated Parmesan cheese**

Following package directions, cook pasta in a large kettle of boiling salted water until al dente. Drain and turn onto a platter; keep warm.

Meanwhile, melt butter in a small pan over low heat. Add basil and parsley and heat until bubbly, then add shrimp and sherry.

Pour shrimp sauce over cooked pasta and sprinkle with salt and Parmesan to taste. Mix gently and serve. Makes 6 to 8 servings.

# MIDSUMMER PASTA

Celebrate the midsummer joy of vine-ripened tomatoes with this quick pasta dish topped with chilled, chopped fresh tomatoes.

**3 tablespoons olive oil or salad oil**
**2 cloves garlic, minced, or pressed**
**1 large onion, coarsely chopped**
**¾ teaspoon salt**
**¼ teaspoon pepper**
**⅛ teaspoon anise seed, crushed**
**1½ teaspoons oregano leaves**
**½ teaspoon *each* dry rosemary and paprika**
**1 cup dry red wine**
**16 ounces rotelle or other large fancy-shaped pasta**
**Boiling salted water**
**2½ pounds (about 6 medium-size) tomatoes, peeled, seeded, and quartered**
**3 or 4 green onions (including tops), thinly sliced**
**½ green pepper, seeded and coarsely chopped**
**Grated Parmesan cheese**

Heat oil in a wide frying pan over medium heat. Add garlic and onion and cook, stirring occasionally, until onion is limp. Add salt, pepper, anise, oregano, rosemary, paprika, and wine. Cover, reduce heat, and simmer for about 15 minutes.

Following package directions, cook pasta in a large kettle of boiling salted water. Drain; then mix with warm onion-wine mixture and turn onto a large platter. Top with tomatoes, onions, and green pepper. Pass Parmesan at the table. Makes 6 to 8 servings.

# Pasta's Close Relatives

## GNOCCHI, SPAETZLE, BEAN THREADS & RICE STICKS

The pasta family is large and global, and some of the offshoots bear little family resemblance to spaghetti, macaroni, noodles, or ravioli. Gnocchi (pronounced nnyah-kee) occupies one such branch of the family tree.

Gnocchi means "lumps," and pasta shaped into lumps and plopped into boiling water is an ancient dish. Made with just flour and water, as it was in an earlier century, gnocchi could be a dull-witted lumpkin of a dish. Indeed, Italians call someone "gnocco" (the singular of gnocchi) when they feel the need to hurl an insult equal to noodlehead, chowderhead, or any of those other food-related epithets common to virtually every language.

But, far from being a noodlehead's dish, gnocchi has been improved by imaginative cooks from its earliest days, when bits of meat and vegetables were pressed into the pasta lumps. Later, cornmeal gnocchi, potato gnocchi, and ricotta gnocchi became popular . . . you'll see why when you try those three versions in this chapter. The cornmeal "lumps" are flavored with bits of cabbage, onion, and cheese; the ricotta gnocchi include spinach and Parmesan for a scrumptious light dumpling; tender potato gnocchi are served with a savory veal sauce.

German spaetzle and its second cousin, kluski, (Polish cream cheese dumplings), are two more European pasta relatives introduced in this chapter.

You make spaetzle by rubbing a thick batter through a colander or spaetzle maker; the result is irregular droplets of pasta that can be sauced or buttered.

On the Far Eastern branch of the pasta family tree, you'll find bean threads and rice sticks, two pasta relatives that look like strands but are made with unusual ingredients—mung beans and rice. Look for them in Oriental markets; you can't make them at home.

In this chapter we include bean thread and rice stick recipes from China, Korea, and the Philippines. You'll find spicy stir-fried dishes, refreshingly crisp salads, and a Chinese chicken soup. Whatever way you present bean threads and rice sticks, they're fascinating dishes.

## CORNMEAL BALL DUMPLINGS

This Italian dumpling is similar to gnocchi but it's not cooked in liquid. Instead, you make a thick cornmeal mush; season it with sautéed cabbage, onion and cheese; then shape the mush into plump balls. Cream keeps the dumplings moist and tender as they heat in the oven.

They go particularly well with scaloppine-type dishes, tomato-flavored stews, and roast turkey or chicken. For a meatless meal, serve the dumplings with a crisp salad, a robust red wine, and wedges of melon and cheese for dessert.

1½ cups finely chopped or shredded cabbage
¼ cup finely chopped onion
¼ cup butter or margarine
1 teaspoon sugar
2 cups water
¾ teaspoon salt
¾ cup yellow cornmeal mixed with ½ cup cold water
½ cup shredded sharp Cheddar cheese
½ cup whipping cream

In a wide frying pan over medium heat, cook cabbage and onion in butter until onion is golden. Stir in sugar.

Bring water and salt to a boil in a 3-quart pan. Stir in cornmeal-water mixture and cook, stirring, over medium-low heat until mush is very thick (about 5 minutes). Stir cabbage mixture into mush. Stir in cheese until it melts.

When mush is cool enough to touch, shape into 1½-inch balls, using about 3 tablespoons mush for each ball. Arrange close together in a greased shallow baking pan. If made ahead, cover and refrigerate until next day.

To heat, pour cream over dumplings, basting each of them. Bake, uncovered, in a 400° oven for about 20 minutes or until tops are lightly browned. Makes 16 dumplings or 3 or 4 main-dish servings.

# POTATO GNOCCHI

Dressed with veal sauce and cheese, or a flavorful tomato sauce, tender potato gnocchi makes a hearty main dish that needs only bread and a green salad as accompaniments. Or you could serve gnocchi as a first course followed by roast beef or chicken and a salad or vegetable dish.

For the best flavor, we feel it's important to make the mashed potatoes from scratch. Once formed into bow tie cylinders, gnocchi should be cooked right away, or frozen and cooked as needed.

**Veal sauce (directions follow)**
**3 cups hot, finely mashed, unseasoned potatoes**
**1½ cups all-purpose flour**
**1½ teaspoons salt**
**1 tablespoon olive oil or salad oil**
**2 eggs, lightly beaten**
**All-purpose flour**
**Boiling salted water**
**2 to 3 tablespoons melted butter**
**1½ cups grated Parmesan or shredded jack cheese, or ¾ pound teleme cheese, thinly sliced**

Make veal sauce. While sauce is simmering, make gnocchi.

Measure hot mashed potatoes into a bowl; add the 1½ cups flour, salt, and oil and blend with a fork. Add eggs and blend thoroughly into potato mixture. Turn potato dough out onto a well-floured board and knead gently about 15 times. If dough is soft, work in a little more flour. Shape into a fat loaf and set on a floured area to prevent sticking.

Cut off one piece of dough (about ½ cup) at a time and roll on a very lightly floured board into a ⅜-inch-thick cord. Cut cord in 1¼-inch lengths and roll each length in the center lightly under your forefinger to give the piece a bow shape. Arrange shaped gnocchi, slightly apart, on a lightly floured cooky sheet.

When all dough is shaped, cook according to directions that follow. Or freeze on the floured cooky sheets until firm, then transfer to plastic bags for longer storage in freezer.

To cook gnocchi, drop about 20 at a time into a large kettle of boiling salted water. Keeping water at a slow boil, cook for 5 minutes (6 minutes, if frozen) after gnocchi return to surface of water. Stir gently if they haven't popped up in about 1 minute.

Remove cooked gnocchi from water with a slotted spoon, draining well. Place cooked gnocchi in a shallow, rimmed pan and mix gently with the melted butter. Cover tightly and place in a warm oven (150°) while you cook remaining gnocchi. They will keep for as long as 1 hour if they are well covered to retain moisture. Flavor is best if they don't cool after cooking.

Arrange half the gnocchi in a layer in a wide, rimmed, ovenproof serving dish and top with half the hot veal sauce and half the cheese. Top with remaining gnocchi, sauce, and cheese. Heat in a 375° oven for about 10 minutes or until cheese melts and gnocchi are piping hot. Broil top lightly if desired. Makes 6 main-dish servings or about 8 first-course servings.

## Veal sauce

**½ cup dried Italian mushrooms**
**¼ cup minced bacon**
**3 tablespoons olive oil**
**¾ pound ground veal**
**1 medium-size onion, finely chopped**
**1 carrot, finely chopped**
**2 stalks celery, finely chopped**
**1 can (about 1 lb.) tomatoes**
**1 can (8 oz.) tomato sauce**
**1 cup dry red wine**
**1½ teaspoons salt**
**⅛ teaspoon pepper**
**¼ teaspoon ground allspice**

Cover mushrooms with warm water; let stand for 30 minutes. Meanwhile, cook bacon in olive oil in a wide frying pan over medium heat until bacon is limp. Add veal, onion, carrot, and celery. Cook, stirring, until veal is browned and vegetables are soft.

Squeeze water from mushrooms, finely chop, and add to meat mixture. Also add tomatoes and their liquid (break up tomatoes with a spoon), tomato sauce, wine, salt, pepper, and allspice. Simmer. uncovered, for 2 hours, stirring occasionally, until sauce is thickened and reduced to about 4 cups. Cool, cover, and refrigerate if made ahead.

# RICOTTA GNOCCHI

Finely chopped spinach colors these light ricotta cheese dumplings. Serve them with melted butter and freshly grated cheese as an accompaniment for meat. Or top the dumplings with a rich tomato-based sauce and serve them as the main dish for a family meal or party buffet.

**Fresh tomato sauce (directions follow)**
**2 packages (10 or 12 oz. each) frozen chopped spinach**
**2 eggs**
**2 cups (1 lb.) ricotta cheese**
**1 cup each fine dry bread crumbs and grated Parmesan cheese**
**1 clove garlic, minced or pressed**
**½ teaspoon salt**
**Dash of pepper**
**¼ teaspoon ground nutmeg**
**1 teaspoon dry basil**
**All-purpose flour**
**Boiling salted water**
**Grated Parmesan cheese**

Prepare fresh tomato sauce.

Cook spinach according to package directions; then drain. When cool enough to handle, press out as much water as possible with your hands.

In a large bowl, beat eggs. Add ricotta and mix well. Stir in bread crumbs, Parmesan, garlic, salt, pepper, nutmeg, basil, and spinach; mix very well. Shape mixture into 1½-inch balls. Roll in flour to coat lightly, and arrange, slightly apart, on a cooky sheet so balls do not touch. If made ahead, cover and refrigerate until next day.

Poach half the balls at a time in a large kettle of boiling salted water. When the water returns to a boil, adjust the heat so the water boils very gently. Cook for 10 minutes. Remove balls with a slotted spoon, drain well, place in a warm serving dish, and keep warm while cooking remainder. Reheat fresh tomato sauce, pour over gnocchi, and sprinkle with Parmesan. Makes 8 servings.

**Fresh tomato sauce.** In a 3-quart pan over medium heat, cook 1 large **onion** (chopped) in 2 tablespoons **butter** or margarine until onion is limp. Add 3 large **tomatoes** (peeled, seeded, and chopped), 1 can (14½ oz.) **chicken broth,** ½ teaspoon *each* **salt** and **dry basil,** and ⅛ teaspoon **pepper.** Bring to a boil over high heat and cook for 10 minutes, stirring occasionally; then reduce heat to medium and continue to cook until reduced to about 2½ cups. Whirl in blender until smooth.

# SPAETZLE

Eggs, flour, and water—the basis of pasta—take a different shape in Austria and Hungary. The ingredients are mixed into a thick batter, then rubbed through a colander or spaetzle maker, causing the batter to break into little droplets as it falls into boiling water. The water firms them almost at once. Spaetzle can be frozen, so you might want to make a good supply.

Serve these dumplings simply mixed with butter, or choose one of the two spaetzle variations that follow.

> 3 eggs
> ½ teaspoon salt
> ½ cup water
> 1¾ cups all-purpose flour
> 2 tablespoons butter or margarine
> Boiling salted water

In a bowl, beat together until very well blended the eggs, salt, water, and flour. Melt butter in a wide pan and keep near cooking area.

Bring a large kettle of boiling salted water to a boil. Place a colander with large holes over the boiling water so that bottom of colander is about 2 inches above

water level. Or hold a spaetzle maker above the water. Ladle about ¼ cup batter into colander or spaetzle maker, then force batter through holes with a rubber spatula so batter falls in droplets into the water.

When spaetzle float to surface (stir if necessary), cook for an additional 10 seconds; then skim spaetzle from water, drain, and place in the pan of melted butter. Shake pan to completely coat spaetzle. Repeat procedure until all batter is used.

Serve buttered spaetzle immediately. Or, if made ahead, cool, cover, and refrigerate for as long as 3 days or freeze for as long as 2 months. Makes 4 to 6 servings.

# SPAETZLE WITH HUNGARIAN SAUCE

Buttery spaetzle cooked with onion, green pepper, and tomato is a perfect accompaniment to bratwurst, garlic sausage, or roast meats.

> 3 tablespoons butter or margarine
> 1 large onion, coarsely chopped
> 1 green pepper, seeded and chopped
> 1 large tomato, peeled, seeded, and chopped
> 1 teaspoon paprika
> 1 recipe cooked spaetzle (recipe at left)
> Salt

In a wide frying pan over medium-high heat, melt butter. Add onion and green pepper and cook until onion is golden. Add tomato and paprika and cook for 3 minutes. Stir in spaetzle and heat through. Season to taste with salt. Makes 4 to 6 servings.

# BROWN BUTTER SPAETZLE

Coated with brown butter and Parmesan cheese, these tiny dumplings make a distinctive side dish to serve with grilled trout or veal chops.

> ¼ cup butter or margarine
> 1 recipe cooked spaetzle (recipe at left)
> ¼ cup grated Parmesan cheese
> 2 tablespoons chopped parsley

Heat butter in a wide frying pan over medium heat until it just begins to brown. Stir in spaetzle and heat through, browning lightly. Sprinkle Parmesan and parsley over spaetzle and gently fold in. Makes 4 to 6 servings.

# KLUSKI

If you were to serve kluski in the Polish or Russian manner, you would ladle thick sour cream over these tangy cream cheese dumplings. If this is too rich for your taste, we suggest two alternatives. You might use the lemon flavoring for the dumplings and serve them with sautéed sole or turbot and a vegetable, such as asparagus, broccoli, or tiny beets. Or you might season them with horseradish and serve with roast or boiled beef.

> 1 large package (8 oz.) cream cheese, softened
> 1 tablespoon butter, softened
> 2 egg yolks
> ½ teaspoon salt
> ¼ cup all-purpose flour
> ½ teaspoon grated lemon peel or prepared horseradish
> 4 tablespoons butter
> Boiling water
> ½ cup fine dry bread crumbs

Blend cream cheese, the 1 tablespoon butter, egg yolks, salt, and flour until smooth. Stir in lemon peel or horseradish. Melt the 4 tablespoons butter in a wide pan and keep near cooking area.

Heat a large kettle of water to a slow boil. Mound about ¼ of dough on a large spoon. Dip a knife blade into hot water and, holding spoon over water, cut off pieces of dough, about 1 teaspoon at a time, and let them drop into the water. Don't worry if dumplings are unevenly shaped. (Dipping knife blade in water helps to release each piece of dough, if necessary.)

When dumplings float to surface, cook for 45 seconds more. Outside of each dumpling should be firm, but inside should still be creamy. Lift from water with a slotted spoon, drain, place in pan of melted butter, and shake pan so dumplings are coated on all sides. Repeat procedure until all batter is used. Shake pan again so dumplings are in a single layer. Sprinkle bread crumbs over dumplings and shake pan gently so they are evenly coated. Turn dumplings into an 8-inch square shallow baking pan. If made ahead, cool, cover, and refrigerate until next day.

To heat, place, uncovered, in a 300° oven for 10 minutes, then set under broiler until tops are lightly browned. Makes 6 servings.

## CHICKEN & SAUSAGE PANSIT

The Filipinos regard pansit in much the same way the Chinese do fried rice—a homey dish that makes good use of small amounts of meats and vegetables. A key ingredient for pansit is rice sticks (also called rice noodles or mai fun).

**6 ounces dried rice sticks**
**3 tablespoons salad oil**
**¼ pound chorizo sausages**
**½ cup chopped onion**
**1 clove garlic, minced or pressed**
**1½ cups diced cooked chicken**
**3 medium-size zucchini, cut in ¼-inch-thick slices**
**¼ cup chicken broth**
**1 tablespoon soy sauce**
**1 egg, lightly beaten**
**1 green onion (including top), minced**

In a bowl, cover rice sticks with warm water and soak for 20 minutes; drain. In a wide frying pan, heat salad oil over medium-high heat. Add rice sticks and cook, stirring, until heated through (about 1 minute). Transfer rice sticks to a platter and keep warm.

Remove and discard casings from chorizos; crumble sausage into pan. Cook, stirring, until browned (about 5 minutes). Discard all but 2 table-spoons of the fat. Add onion, garlic, and chicken to pan; cook until onion is limp. Stir in zucchini, chicken broth, and soy sauce, then cover and cook for 3 minutes.

Remove pan from heat. With a fork, lightly stir in egg just until set. Spoon mixture over rice sticks. Sprinkle with green onion. Makes 3 or 4 servings.

## CHICKEN WITH SHINING NOODLES SOUP

Bean threads, one of the most unusual pastas used in Oriental cooking, are actually noodles in disguise. Because they are made from mung beans rather than from flour and water, they are considered a vegetable product, though Oriental cooks use them as pasta—in soups and stir-fried with meats or vegetables. Look for the black bean seasoning in Oriental markets.

**4 ounces dried bean threads**
**2 teaspoons *each* cornstarch, dry sherry, and salad oil**
**1 pound chicken breasts, skinned, boned, and cut in bite-size pieces**
**3 tablespoons fermented black beans**
**2 tablespoons salad oil**
**1 tablespoon minced garlic**
**3 to 6 small, dry, whole hot chile peppers**
**6 cups chicken broth**
**1 tablespoon soy sauce**
**1½ teaspoons sugar**
**3 green onions (including tops), cut in 2-inch lengths**
**1 teaspoon sesame oil**
**Salt**

Cover bean threads with warm water and let stand for 30 minutes. Drain, then cut in 6-inch lengths. In a bowl, blend cornstarch, sherry, and the 2 teaspoons oil. Add chicken and mix well; let stand for 10 minutes. Rinse black beans and drain.

In a 3-quart pan, heat the 2 tablespoons oil over medium-low heat. Add black beans, garlic, and whole chile peppers. Cook, stirring, until spices smell fragrant and begin to brown (1 to 2 minutes); do not allow spices to burn. Add chicken broth, soy, sugar, and bean threads. Bring to a boil, then reduce heat and simmer, uncovered, for 5 minutes.

Stir in chicken and onions and cook, stirring occasionally, until chicken is opaque (about 3 minutes). Just before serving, stir in sesame oil and season to taste with salt. Remove whole chiles as you ladle soup into a tureen. Makes 6 servings.

## PORK & SHRIMP PANSIT

The cooking of this one-dish meal is fast-paced, so be sure to have all the ingredients ready and close at hand to use in sequence.

**6 ounces dried rice sticks**
**5 tablespoons salad oil**
**1 small onion, chopped**
**1 teaspoon minced fresh ginger**
**2 cloves garlic, minced or pressed**
**1½ cups *each* diced cooked pork (such as roast or chops) and small cooked shrimp**
**4 cups lightly packed shredded bok choy or Swiss chard**
**3 tablespoons oyster sauce or 2 tablespoons soy sauce**
**¼ cup chicken broth**
**¼ teaspoon crushed red pepper**
**1 green onion (including top), minced**

In a bowl, cover rice sticks with warm water and soak for 20 minutes; drain.

In a wide frying pan, heat 3 table-spoons of the oil over medium-high heat. Add rice sticks and cook, stirring, until heated through (about 1 minute). Transfer rice sticks to a platter and keep warm.

Heat remaining 2 tablespoons oil in pan over high heat. Add onion, ginger, garlic, pork, and shrimp. Cook, stirring, for 1 minute. Stir in bok choy, oyster sauce, chicken broth, and red pepper, then cover and cook for 1 minute or until greens wilt. Spoon mixture over rice sticks. Sprinkle with green onion. Makes 3 or 4 servings.

## SPICY BEAN THREADS

The Chinese serve noodle dishes as quick snacks the way Italians serve pizza. Here is one made with bean threads and flecked with bits of pork.

**2 ounces dried bean threads**
**2 medium-size dried Oriental mushrooms**
**3 tablespoons salad oil**
**1 teaspoon minced fresh ginger**
**2 cloves garlic, minced or pressed**
**2 ounces ground lean pork**
**1 or 2 small, dry, hot chile peppers, crumbled**
**1 green onion (including top), thinly sliced**
**½ cup chicken broth**
**1 tablespoon** *each* **dry sherry and soy sauce**
**1 teaspoon sesame oil**

Cover bean theads with warm water and let stand for 30 minutes. Drain, then cut in 4-inch lengths. Cover mushrooms with warm water, let stand for 30 minutes, then drain. Cut off and discard stems; squeeze water from mushrooms and thinly slice.

Heat a wide frying pan over high heat. When pan is hot, add oil. When oil begins to heat, add ginger and garlic. Stir once, then add pork and chiles. Cook, stirring, until pork loses its pinkness (about 2 minutes). Reduce heat to medium.

Add mushrooms, bean threads, onion, chicken broth, sherry, and soy. Stirring occasionally, simmer until all liquid is absorbed (about 5 minutes). Stir in sesame oil just before serving. Makes 4 servings.

## KOREAN BEEF & BEAN THREADS

Tender meat strips, crisp vegetables, and silky bean threads—here's a complete one-step meal to cook in a wok. If you wish to extend it to four servings, serve it with steamed rice and—Korean-style—small side dishes of pickled kim chee, available in Oriental markets.

**3 ounces dried bean threads**
**3 medium-size dried Oriental mushrooms**
**3 tablespoons sesame seeds**
**¾ pound boneless lean beef**
**1 tablespoon sesame oil**
**¼ teaspoon pepper**
**½ teaspoon crushed red pepper**
**2 cloves garlic, minced or pressed**
**2 tablespoons soy sauce**
**3 tablespoons salad oil**
**1 small green pepper, seeded and cut in thin strips**
**1 medium-size carrot, shredded**
**6 green onions (including tops), cut in 2-inch lengths**
**¼ pound bean sprouts**
**⅓ cup beef broth**
**¾ teaspoon salt**
**1 teaspoon** *each* **sugar and vinegar**

Cover bean threads with warm water and let stand for 30 minutes. Drain, then cut in 2-inch lengths. Cover mushrooms with warm water, let stand for 30 minutes, then drain. Cut off and discard stems; squeeze water from mushrooms and thinly slice. In a small pan, cook sesame seeds over low heat, shaking pan occasionally, until golden (about 2 minutes).

Cut beef with the grain into 1½-inch-wide strips. Cut each strip across the grain in ⅛-inch-thick slanting slices. In a bowl, combine sesame oil, pepper, crushed red pepper, garlic, and 1 tablespoon of the soy. Add beef and stir to coat.

Heat a wok or wide frying pan over high heat. When pan is hot, add 1 tablespoon of the salad oil. When oil is hot, add beef and stir-fry until meat is browned on the outside but still pink within (about 1½ minutes); remove meat from pan.

Heat remaining 2 tablespoons salad oil. Add green pepper, carrot, mushrooms, onions, and bean sprouts. Stir-fry for 2 minutes. Remove from pan.

Add broth, salt, sugar, vinegar, remaining 1 tablespoon soy, and bean theads to pan. Cook, stirring frequently, until liquid is absorbed (about 2 minutes). Return meat and vegetables to pan and stir in 2 tablespoons of the sesame seeds. Turn onto a serving platter and sprinkle with remaining 1 tablespoon sesame seeds. Makes 3 or 4 servings.

## SILVER THREAD STIRRED EGGS

Silky bean threads give a bouncy lightness to scrambled eggs laced with meat and vegetables. This would be a good brunch or luncheon dish.

**2 ounces dried bean threads**
**4 medium-size dried Oriental mushrooms**
**2 teaspoons soy sauce**
**6 eggs**
**½ teaspoon salt**
**⅛ teaspoon white pepper**
**2 tablespoons salad oil**
**1 clove garlic, minced or pressed**
**4 ounces cooked ham, diced**
**1 stalk celery, thinly sliced**
**¼ cup sliced bamboo shoots**
**2 green onions (including tops), thinly sliced**

Cover bean threads with warm water and let stand for 30 minutes. Drain, then cut in 4-inch lengths.

Cover mushrooms with ¾ cup warm water and let stand for 30 minutes. Remove mushrooms from water and set aside. Pour ½ cup of the water into a bowl; discard sandy water that remains. Add soy to mushroom water. Cut off and discard mushroom stems; squeeze water from mushrooms and slice thinly. In a bowl, beat eggs with salt and pepper.

Heat a wide frying pan over high heat. When pan is hot, add oil. When oil begins to heat, add garlic. Stir once, then add ham and mushrooms and cook, stirring, for 1 minute. Add celery and bamboo shoots and cook for 2 minutes. Add bean threads and mushroom water and cook until liquid is absorbed. Add green onion and cook for 30 seconds. Reduce heat to medium and pour eggs into pan. Turning occasionally with a wide spatula, cook eggs until they are soft and creamy. Makes 4 servings.

## DEEP-FRIED BEAN THREADS & RICE STICKS

Dried bean threads and rice sticks perform like no other pasta—when dropped into hot fat, they puff and expand, changing from wiry strands to crinkly, crunchy noodles.

In Chinese cooking, these crisp fried noodles are used as a garnish —notably in Chinese-style salads, like the two recipes that follow. You can deep-fry the noodles ahead of time. Stored in an airtight container, they will keep at room temperature for several weeks.

Bean threads and rice sticks are packaged in tight bundles and are messy to separate. To avoid scattering, place a bundle in a large paper bag, then pull the bundle apart into small sections or individual strands.

Pour salad oil into a wok or deep pan to a depth of 2 inches and heat to 375° on a deep-frying thermometer. Drop in one bean thread or rice stick. If it expands at once, the oil is ready. Cook a small handful at a time. As noodles puff and expand, push them down into the oil with a wire strainer or slotted spoon, then turn over the entire mass to be sure all are cooked. When noodles stop crackling (about 30 seconds), remove with a strainer and drain on paper towels.

## CHINESE CHICKEN SALAD

Crinkly strands of crisp-fried bean threads are one of the hallmarks of this classic Chinese salad. Mix them in at the last minute, after you have mixed in the piquant lemon flavored salad dressing, so they will retain their crispness.

> 2 tablespoons soy sauce
> 1 tablespoon *each* salad oil and dry sherry
> 1 clove garlic, minced or pressed
> ¼ teaspoon ground ginger
> ¼ teaspoon Chinese five-spice or ground cinnamon
> 2½ to 3-pound broiler-fryer, cut in half
> ¼ cup sesame seeds
>   About 6 cups thinly shredded iceberg lettuce
> 3 green onions (including tops), thinly sliced
> ½ cup coarsely chopped fresh coriander (also called Chinese parsley or cilantro)
> ½ cup chopped salted cashews or peanuts
>   Lemon dressing (directions follow)
>   Salt and pepper
> 2 to 3 cups deep-fried bean threads or rice sticks (directions at left)

Mix together soy, salad oil, sherry, garlic, ginger, and five-spice. Rub mixture over chicken halves, coating thoroughly. Place chicken, skin side up, in a shallow baking pan. Pour over any extra soy mixture. Bake in a 400° oven until meat near bone is no longer pink when slashed (about 45 minutes); cool. Skin and bone chicken and cut meat into thin strips.

Spread sesame seeds in a pan and cook over low heat, shaking pan occasionally, until seeds turn golden and begin to pop (about 2 minutes); let cool.

In a salad bowl, mix together chicken, lettuce, onion, coriander, sesame seeds, and nuts. Prepare lemon dressing, pour over chicken mixture, and toss lightly. Add salt and pepper to taste. Add fried bean threads and mix lightly. Serve immediately. Makes 6 servings.

**Lemon dressing.** In a bowl, combine ½ teaspoon **dry mustard**, 1 teaspoon *each* **sugar** and **grated lemon peel**, 2 teaspoons **soy sauce**, 1 tablespoon **lemon juice**, and 4 tablespoons **salad oil**.

## ORIENTAL SHRIMP SALAD

A sweet and sour dressing puts the finishing touch on this quick variation of the classic Chinese chicken salad. Fresh coriander is a pungent herb—adjust the quantity to suit your taste.

>   Oriental dressing (directions follow)
> 3 to 4 cups shredded iceberg lettuce
> 3 green onions (including tops), thinly sliced
> 1 large carrot, coarsely shredded
> ½ pound small cooked shrimp or 2 cans (4½ oz. *each*) small cooked shrimp, drained
> ¼ to ½ cup coarsely chopped fresh coriander (also called Chinese parsley or cilantro)
>   Salt and pepper
> 2 to 3 cups deep-fried bean threads or rice sticks (directions at left)

Prepare Oriental dressing.

In a salad bowl, place lettuce, green onion, carrot, shrimp, and coriander. Cover and refrigerate until serving time.

Just before serving, pour over dressing and mix lightly. Season with salt and pepper to taste. Add fried bean threads and mix lightly; serve immediately. Makes 6 servings.

**Oriental dressing.** Spread 2 teaspoons **sesame seeds** in a pan and cook over low heat, shaking pan occasionally, until seeds turn golden and begin to pop (about 2 minutes). In a bowl, mix 4 tablespoons **white wine vinegar**, 3 tablespoons **sugar**, 1 tablespoon **salad oil**, 1 teaspoon *each* grated **lemon peel** and **soy sauce**, and the toasted sesame seeds.

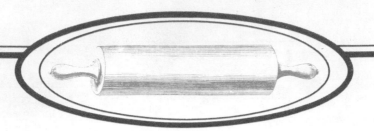

# PASTA PARTY! PASTA PARTY!

This party has built-in entertainment—a hand-crank or electric pasta machine. It's a fun party to stage because pasta-making inspires conviviality. And with some advance planning and cooking, you'll be able to join in the activity, too, and have fun cranking out the noodles.

By nature, a pasta party is casual, so warn people that they'll be playing with flour and should dress accordingly. You might even want to provide chefs' aprons or large tea towels as cover-ups.

To launch the pasta-making, offer your guests a round of antipasto and wine, then give a brief demonstration of rolling out and cutting noodles. Invite your guests to work in pairs: they can take turns rolling out the dough strips, then one person can cut the noodles while the other catches them as they are cranked through the pasta machine. The rest of your guests can kibitz while waiting their turns.

## PLANNING AHEAD

Since fresh noodles taste so good, and everyone has a hand in preparation, plan on people consuming more than they would ordinarily. For four people, figure one batch of dough, such as all-purpose pasta (page 8), cut into medium-wide noodles. Make two separate batches for five to eight people. That's as large a quantity of noodles as you'll want to cook. In fact, your guest list really is limited by the amount of pasta you can cook and serve at one time. An enormous quantity of pasta is difficult to cook and unwieldy to serve.

Have doughs mixed, kneaded, and resting before your guests arrive. By the way, it's not considered cheating to roll out part of the dough before the party starts—especially if you're making two batches.

Select only sauces that can be made ahead and reheated, or sauces that can be assembled quickly while the pasta is being cut. Two sauces are plenty. Here are some winning duos: pine nut sauce (page 17) and sausage tomato sauce (page 68); rapido sauce (page 17) and crispy-meat sauce (page 23); basil and tomato sauce (page 23) and quattro formaggi sauce (page 20).

Some sauces have to be tossed with the noodles before serving; others can be served in bowls for guests to help themselves.

## ANTIPASTO IDEAS

There is no set way to prepare or serve antipasto, the Italian equivalent of appetizers. You can arrange a large platter of tasty morsels purchased at an Italian grocery or delicatessen. This might include cold cuts, such as fine salami, imported prosciutto, zampino, mortadella, and galantina; mixed pickled vegetables, called giardiniera; pepperoncini; anchovies; a chunk of hard cheese such as Parmesan, or a chunk of soft cheese such as teleme; and black and green olives. Other top-rated candidates for antipasto include French bread or bread sticks, jack cheese, raw celery, radishes, carrots, or fresh tomatoes with basil Parmesan (page 21). Or you can make one or more of the recipes that follow.

Finger-foods, or antipasto set out smorgasbord-style, works much better than a sit-down first course. Have plenty of small plates on hand, so guests can help themselves easily.

## ANTIPASTO SALAD

- ½ small head cauliflower
- 1 head *each* red lettuce and curly endive, torn into bite-size pieces
- 1 can (1 lb.) red kidney beans, drained
- 1 can (1 lb.) garbanzos, drained
- 2 green onions (including tops), chopped
- 1 can (2¼ oz.) sliced ripe olives, drained
- ½ cup olive oil
- ¼ cup vinegar
- ¾ teaspoon salt
- ⅛ teaspoon pepper
- 2 tomatoes, sliced
- 1 can (2 oz.) anchovy fillets, drained
- 2 hard-cooked eggs, sliced

Break cauliflower into flowerets and parboil just until slightly tender; drain and cool. In a large salad bowl, combine cauliflower, greens, kidney beans, garbanzos, onions, and olives. Chill until ready to serve.

Make a dressing of the olive oil, vinegar, salt, and pepper. When ready to serve, toss salad with dressing and garnish with tomatoes, anchovies, and sliced eggs. Makes 8 to 10 servings.